Teaching with Emotional Intelligence

The way teacher ... ir learners is central to the s ... ow in its second edition, *Teaching with Emotional Intelligence* shows how to manage this influential yet neglected area of learning and teaching. This practical book looks at how lecturers and teachers can develop and use their emotional intelligence to enhance their teaching and their students' learning.

Taking the reader step-by-step through the learning process and looking at the relationship from the perspective of both the teacher and the learner, this book will help the reader to:

- plan the emotional environment;
- learn how to relate and listen to learners effectively;
- read and respond to the feelings of individuals and groups;
- handle and reveal their feelings as a teacher, as appropriate;
- develop self-awareness as a teacher;
- recognize their prejudices and preferences;
- improve non-verbal communication;
- plan for the physical experience of learners;
- deal with their learners' expectations, comments and questions.

This book contains a number of revised activities, checklists and points for deeper reflection as well as new chapters on teaching with emotional intelligence with international students, in online learning and in working one-to-one with students. It will help all teaching professionals encourage their learners to become more engaged, creative, positive and motivated.

Alan Mortiboys has over 20 years' experience working in Educational Development in Higher Education, most recently as Professor of Educational Development at Birmingham City University. He now works independently, providing staff and educational development for professionals in education and healthcare.

For Daniel

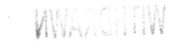

Teaching with Emotional Intelligence

A step by step guide for
higher and further education
professionals

Second edition

Alan Mortiboys

Routledge
Taylor & Francis Group

LONDON AND NEW YORK

First edition published 2005
by Routledge

This second edition published 2012
by Routledge
2 Park Square, Milton Park, Abingdon, Oxon OX14 4RN

Simultaneously published in the USA and Canada
by Routledge
711 Third Avenue, New York, NY 10017

Routledge is an imprint of the Taylor & Francis Group, an informa business

British Library Cataloguing in Publication Data
A catalogue record for this book is available from the British Library

Library of Congress Cataloging in Publication Data
Mortiboys, Alan.
Teaching with emotional intelligence : a step-by-step guide for higher and further education professionals / Alan Mortiboys. -- 2nd ed.
p. cm.
Includes bibliographical references and index.
1. Affective education. 2. Emotional intelligence. 3. Emotions and cognition. 4. College teaching. 5. Adult education. I. Title.
LB1072.M67 2011
374--dc22
2011005291

ISBN: 978-0-415-57138-8 (hbk)
ISBN: 978-0-415-57140-1 (pbk)
ISBN: 978-0-203-80646-3 (ebk)

Typeset in Galliard
by Saxon Graphics Ltd, Derby

Printed and bound in Great Britain by
TJ International Ltd, Padstow, Cornwall

Contents

Acknowledgements

Thanks once more to colleagues and to the many participants in workshops I have run on teaching with emotional intelligence, whose comments have helped greatly in shaping the content of this book.

Thanks for help and advice from: Matt Badcock, Kathy Burrell, Jude Carroll, Dennis Foster, Jim Judges and Janette Ryan.

Thanks to Mary for style and inspiration.

Preface to the second edition

Teaching with Emotional Intelligence was first published in 2005. Since then, I have run workshops, given keynotes and contributed short sessions on the subject on over 100 occasions. Most of these sessions have been very interactive and I have heard many comments, suggestions, challenges and questions from participants. These have been invaluable in the revision and some expansion of existing chapters. There are also three new chapters in this edition, each of which begins to answer the question of to what extent the ideas in the original book can be applied in a particular context: working with a learner one-to-one, in online learning, and with international students. For these new chapters, I have sought to maintain a practical focus, referring back to activities in earlier chapters, as well as offering new suggestions specific to that context.

Activities

Introduction

The emotional dimension of learning and teaching

I have run a number of workshops on teaching with emotional intelligence in which I have begun by asking participants to think of an occasion when they were a learner that aroused in them strong feelings. After everyone has had the chance to remember such an occasion and to briefly recount their experience to a partner, I ask individuals to state the word or phrase that captures the strong feeling they are recalling. These are examples of the words they use in their responses: anger, resentment, excitement, frustration, embarrassment, inadequacy, helplessness, fear, relief, outrage. The ratio of 'negative' to 'positive' feelings is usually the same as in this selection.

Participants in these workshops include teachers (from higher education, further education, adult education and schools) and healthcare professionals involved in teaching, who have been relatively successful in their experience of formal education. I gather these responses at the workshops for the same reason that I repeat them now. It is to set the scene, by acknowledging what we all know intuitively from our own experience: that emotions are bound up with learning. In Guy Claxton's words: 'Learning itself is an intrinsically emotional business' (Claxton 1999: 15). The process of learning in any context can involve struggle, frustration, thrill or excitement. In the public and formal context of the classroom, with all of the dynamics between teacher and learner and among learners, and with the perception that there is the prospect of success or failure, the potential for strong feelings is heightened. Although the strong feelings that are recalled by participants in this exercise may not be typical of an everyday class, where there is learning there are likely to be emotions. In the words of Daniel Liston,

> we have no choice but to recognize the emotional contours of teaching and learning. Ignoring those dimensions won't make them go away. In learning and teaching, emotions are ever present. Ignoring or suppressing those emotions harms students and teachers alike.
>
> (Liston 2003: 115–16)

It appears that learners' emotions have an effect on their learning and also that the teacher has a significant role to play in shaping those emotions. Sarah Moore and Nyiel Kuol analysed the responses of past students at the University of Limerick who were asked to explain their nomination of a lecturer for a teaching award. They found that: 'students often refer to emotions, emotional states and emotionally satisfying experiences when providing descriptions of excellent teaching and generally seem to associate their own and their teachers' positive emotional states with good teaching and good learning' (Moore and Kuol 2007: 87).

John Dirkx writes that participants on his teaching courses,

> in recalling incidents of memorable learning ... typically describe experiences in which there was a strong, positive, emotional or affective dimension, such as a supportive climate, a caring teacher who listens to us as individuals, a teacher who respects us as persons, or a teacher who involves the whole person in the learning experience.
>
> (Dirkx 2001: 67)

Debra Meyer and Julianne Turner discuss how, in their many studies of motivation and learning, emotion has emerged as an 'integral part of the interpersonal processes that create classroom contexts' (Meyer and Turner 2002: 107). They observe that 'cognitive support is necessary but not sufficient for learning experiences to evoke student involvement' (ibid.: 111). It is the teacher's demonstration of positive emotions and motivation as learners that correlates with student reports of positive affect and motivation to learn (ibid.: 112).

It follows that if the goal of a teacher is to help their learners to learn, a teacher needs to be able to recognize the emotional dimension of learning and to work with it. This includes acknowledging that there are things within the control of the individual teacher that can affect how learners feel (whilst recognizing of course that the teacher is not the only influence on learners' feelings).

Emotional intelligence

So, given the power and inevitability of emotions in learning and teaching and the influence on learners' feelings that can be exerted by the teacher, it is essential to ask what it is that the teacher needs to have and to develop in order to maximize the potential for emotions to support rather than hinder learning. 'Emotional intelligence' is a useful term to use to encapsulate this.

The term emotional intelligence was popularized by the success of Daniel Goleman's book *Emotional Intelligence: Why it can matter more than IQ*, which appeared in 1995 (1996 in the UK). Goleman defined emotional intelligence or 'EQ' as 'the capacity for recognizing our own feelings and those of others, for motivating ourselves, and for managing emotions well in ourselves and in our relationships' (Goleman 1998: 317). The term 'emotional intelligence' was coined in 1990 by Jack Mayer and Peter Salovey. By 1997, they stated that emotional intelligence involves:

- the ability to perceive accurately, appraise and express emotion;
- the ability to access and/or generate feelings when they facilitate thought;
- the ability to understand emotions and emotional knowledge;
- the ability to regulate emotions to promote emotional and intellectual growth.

(Salovey and Mayer 1997: 10)

Goleman's book created a great deal of interest in the concept of 'emotional intelligence'. Businesses asked, 'How can we develop emotional intelligence at work so that the company can be more successful?' and 'How do we measure emotional intelligence in prospective employees?' Parents and schoolteachers asked, 'How can we develop emotional intelligence in our children to enable them to lead happier and more successful lives?' What I believe has been overlooked in the interest generated by Goleman's book is the vital role that the use of emotional intelligence can play in teaching.

Conventionally, a teacher brings two things to the classroom that are of value to the learners. One is expertise in the subject, derived from study, research or professional experience. The other is knowledge of learning and teaching methods – a teacher's pedagogy, such as how to structure the content being presented, how to encourage participation by learners, use of materials and so on. I suggest that emotional intelligence is the unrecognized third component of what a teacher should be able to offer to learners. I believe that, as teachers, we should develop and employ emotional intelligence to complement the subject expertise and pedagogical skills that we already offer to learners. When you are with a group of learners, you have the chance to connect with them beyond the transmission and discussion of ideas and facts, and thereby to transform the experience both for you and for them. If you do not use emotional intelligence in your teaching, the value of both your knowledge of your subject and your learning and teaching methods can be seriously diminished. This is represented in the diagram below.

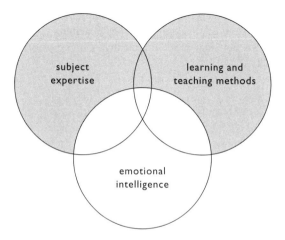

Using emotional intelligence has the potential to affect for the better many aspects of your work as a teacher. For example, many problems with 'discipline' can be attributed to how teachers respond to (or ignore) learners' feelings (see Chapter 9); learners may be less likely to drop out from courses if they have better relationships with teachers (see chapters 2 and 6); and for effective reflective learning to occur, the use of emotional intelligence is a prerequisite (see Chapter 18). Above all, the teacher who pays attention to the emotional dimension of the classroom experience is more likely to develop a state in their learners which is conducive to learning (see Chapter 3), with an increased likelihood of learners being engaged, motivated, confident, constructive, ready to collaborate, creative and resilient.

How emotions are overlooked in learning and teaching

Currently, however, many teachers are unlikely even to recognize the emotional dimension of their work. This has been made very apparent to me in the course of carrying out teaching observations in a range of contexts in post-16 learning. I have frequently seen teachers who were very competent in their teaching skills but who simply did not pay attention to the emotional dimension of the learning–teaching exchange. For example, they might not address any student by name, even though the group was small enough for them to know the name of each learner. Or they never explicitly acknowledged the look of boredom or confusion on the faces of some group members. Opportunities were lost for promoting a positive emotional environment and for responding to the feelings of learners, in order to enhance the experience both for the teacher and for their learners.

Emotions still appear to be marginalized in further and higher education. John Heron suggests one reason for this:

> if a disease model or treatment model of working on feelings is adopted, then professional helpers of all kinds – from teachers to doctors – exempt themselves from personal work on feelings on the grounds that they are normal, not ill.
>
> (Heron 1982: 36)

If emotions only merit attention, and then in the form of treatment, when they are perceived as a problem, it will not be possible to acknowledge and engage with their everyday presence in learning and teaching. In this view, emotions are pathologized.

Another cause of the continued neglect of this vital component of learning and teaching is the perception that emotions are an obstacle to reason. This can be attributed to the enduring influence of the writings of René Descartes. In the seventeenth century Descartes wrote, 'I think therefore I am.' He stated that each of us has a 'mental' realm within us which is uncontaminated by the sensual nature of the body. This separate realm of the mind was seen as 'higher' than the faculties of the body, which was closer to animal nature. This model continues to influence much of education today, as the intellect is seen as the location of rational thought and, therefore, more trustworthy than the emotions. As Anne Brockbank and Ian McGill note, '[Descartes'] dualism . . . has survived in almost all aspects of learning and development, as can be seen in the preoccupation with "thinking skills" to the exclusion of material factors like affect (emotion) and action' (Brockbank and McGill 1998: 21). If learning is seen as purely a cognitive process, it is legitimate for the teacher to confine their energies to asking the right questions, providing information and ideas, demonstrating skills, orchestrating learner discussion and so on. In his book *Descartes' Error,* Antonio Damasio has shown that, from a neuroscientist's perspective, Descartes was wrong. He demonstrates the central role of emotions in decision-making and asserts that 'certain aspects of the process of emotion and feelings are indispensable for rationality' (Damasio 1996: xv).

Both of these views, seeing emotions as pathological and as anti-reason, still attract support, as evidenced, for instance, in Katherine Ecclestone and Dennis Hayes's recent book, *The Dangerous Rise of Therapeutic Education* (2009). However, it is time to recognize the central role that emotions play in learning and to ensure that using emotional intelligence is part of every teacher's development. This is particularly needed in higher education. As Patricia Owen-Smith warns, it does not mean 'over-romanticising the emotional and reducing the material of our courses and our disciplines to secondary stature' (Owen-Smith 2008: 2). It does not necessitate sacrificing a higher education which values and fosters coherent critical argument, independence of thought and academic rigour but, rather, recognizing that these aspects can be enriched by infusing them with humanity. The university is indeed the 'home of reason', but reason is bound up with emotion, not distinct from it. It is possible to respect the feelings of learners at the same time as vigorously challenging their ideas. The use of emotional intelligence by teachers is not a threat to, but more an essential component of, university education.

Teaching with emotional intelligence in practice

The emphasis in this book is on using your emotional intelligence as a teacher to attend to the emotional dimension of learning and teaching. I suggest that as a teacher you should develop and use your emotional intelligence with two goals in mind.

- One is to be able to recognize and respond to the feelings of both yourself and your learners in the classroom, in order to make you both more effective in your respective roles.

• The second is to encourage an emotional state in the learners on your course that is conducive to learning. This can apply just as much to the two-hour workshop as to the course which runs for the whole year.

This book is concerned with what it means in practice to work towards these goals. Each of the many activities throughout the book is intended to help you achieve one or both of them.

Of course, when you look more closely at what is meant by the use of emotional intelligence in teaching you may say, 'I do this anyway – this is just a name I can put to it.' For many, the concept of emotional intelligence embodies a description of how they live their life, including their teaching, and they will be doing this as a matter of course. They will see that all people, including those in the role of learner, have feelings and that those feelings deserve to be acknowledged, valued, respected and handled with care. If you are one of those who already teach with emotional intelligence, I would say that there is still more to do:

• first, we can rescue emotional intelligence from being an extra quality that a minority of teachers offer to learners. Instead, it deserves to be recognized as an essential component of what all teachers should offer;
• secondly, rather than let the use of emotional intelligence be just intuitive, we should be more deliberate in using it, for example, in planning (see chapters 3–5);
• thirdly, we should give the use of emotional intelligence as much attention as we give to content and methods; we should give it a greater share of our energy.

This book is intended as a practical guide for teachers who wish to make more use of emotional intelligence in their teaching. Throughout, the emphasis is on helping you as a teacher to relate the detail of emotional intelligence to the context in which you work, and to assist you in developing your own emotional intelligence and your use of it with your learners.

Outline of the book

With the exception of chapters 1, 15, 16 and 17, each chapter takes a different aspect of teaching with emotional intelligence and is in three parts:

1. *What does it mean and why does it matter?*
   Explores that chapter's particular aspect of teaching with emotional intelligence, what it means for your practice and what effect its use can have.

2. *Investigating your practice*
   Provides an opportunity for you to review your current use of this aspect of teaching with emotional intelligence.

3. *Developing your practice*
   Provides suggestions on how you could introduce or further develop this aspect in your teaching.

The *Investigating your practice* and *Developing your practice* sections of each chapter consist primarily of a number of 'activities'. The aims of these activities vary. They may be: for developing your skills in the use of, and/or your understanding of, teaching with emotional intelligence; for reviewing your practice; inviting you to make speculative plans for your teaching; offering suggestions for you to use in a session or for developing your self-awareness.

Chapter 1 explores further what is meant by the term 'emotional intelligence' in teaching. Chapter 2 invites you to investigate the nature of your relationship with learners. Chapters 3–5 are about planning for the use of emotional intelligence in your teaching whilst chapters 6–9 are about using emotional intelligence in your exchanges with learners in the classroom, which involves being alert to opportunities presented and making the most of them. Chapters 10–12 focus on developing your self-awareness as a teacher, chapters 13 and 14 are about shaping, handling and revealing your feelings, and Chapter 18 looks at how you can continue your development in teaching with emotional intelligence. Chapters 15, 16 and 17 are new to this second edition. They ask how far the ideas presented in earlier chapters can be applied:

- when working one-to-one with a learner;
- in online learning and teaching;
- when teaching international students.

It is possible to do all of the activities in this book by working alone. However, you would derive greater benefit from exploring them with one or more colleagues. The majority of them may be adapted as activities on courses and indeed many have been used in this way.

The book is intended to be of use to both new and experienced teachers. The activities and examples assume that you are working with learners aged 16 or over, although the principles behind the use of emotional intelligence can apply to teachers of all ages of learner. I have used the term 'teacher' throughout for the role that you may know as lecturer, tutor, teacher, trainer or facilitator. Equally, for the people whom you are teaching, whether you call them students, participants, delegates or even pupils, I am using the term 'learners' (except in Chapter 17, when discussing 'international students'). The space in which you meet I am calling a 'classroom' and the time you spend with them, a 'session'.

Chapter 1

The emotionally intelligent teacher

This chapter includes the following activities:

1.1 The qualities of an emotionally intelligent teacher
1.2 Providing evidence of the use of emotional intelligence
1.3 Planning for the feelings you wish to generate in your learners
1.4 Being present

What is an emotionally intelligent teacher? How would you know one if you saw one? The chapter titles in the rest of this book give you a sense of what it means to teach with emotional intelligence. This includes: creating a positive emotional climate; recognizing and working with the feelings of yourself and of your learners; using listening skills with groups as well as with individuals; dealing with learners' expectations; and having a developed self-awareness.

Research into desirable teacher attributes identifies characteristics of emotional intelligence in teachers without necessarily giving them that name. Joe Harkin reported on vocational education learners aged 17–19 and found that: 'affective behaviours are the most important determinants of student satisfaction with teachers . . . [These behaviours include] recognizing individuals, listening to students, showing respect, being friendly, sharing a joke, making some self-disclosure' (Harkin 1998: 339, 346).

One of the outstanding teachers interviewed by Cynthia Weston and Lynn McAlpine says, 'it is how much you care rather than how much you know; caring is very significant' (Weston and McAlpine 1998: 147). This echoes the findings of Sarah Moore and Nyiel Kuol (see page 2) – 'who a teacher is with their students seemed to be more relevant to this group of respondents than what a teacher does with his/her subject' (Moore and Kuol 2007: 90).

Barbara Harrell Carson gathered the responses of former students, who graduated over a period of 26 years from Rollins College in Orlando, about teachers whom they perceived to be most effective. She found that 'the single quality the Rollins alumni most frequently associated with effective teachers – more often than brilliance and love of subject and even more often than enthusiasm in the classroom – was a special attitude toward and relationship with students' (Carson 1996: 14). The respondents 'connected their transformative experiences . . . with a complex and personal encounter linking professor, student, and subject matter in an exchange as much affective as cognitive' (ibid.: 11).

Activities 1.1 and 1.2, which follow later in this chapter, invite you to explore further the characteristics of emotionally intelligent teachers.

Teaching with emotional intelligence entails a shift in priorities. For example, the emotionally intelligent teacher seeks to have confidence not just in their content and materials but also in their flexibility and readiness to respond; they put energy into planning a teaching session but also into preparing to meet the learners; they see their self-development as emphasizing not just subject expertise but also the development of their self-knowledge.

In other words, emotionally intelligent teachers distribute their energies differently. With reference to the diagram on page 3, they put at least as much energy into using and developing emotional intelligence as into maintaining their subject expertise and developing their pedagogical skills. This means always being aware of how the affective intertwines with the cognitive in learning and in their teaching, and ensuring that what they say and do always has an eye to influencing or responding to feelings, both on their part and on the part of the learners. This includes being both proactive and reactive: proactive as in activity 1.3 which follows and in most of the activities in chapters 2 to 5, which are about planning; reactive as in the sense of being alert for opportunities to attend to feelings and seizing them, such as when responding to learners' comments. This is reflected in activity 1.4 which follows and in most activities in chapters 6 to 9.

Developing as an emotionally intelligent teacher

In the workshops I run on teaching with emotional intelligence, I occasionally receive the comment, 'I agree that emotional intelligence is important, but surely you are talking about a personal quality, which you either do or do not possess. It cannot be learnt.' I am convinced that it can be learnt. Anyone with experience of teaching or learning on counselling skills courses, for example, will know that some individuals have the capacity to change both their interpersonal behaviours and how they view themselves and others; that is, to develop their emotional intelligence.

If you are seeking to develop your use of emotional intelligence as a teacher, it is worth reflecting on just what it is that you are looking to change and how that change will come about. A first potential trap in developing emotional intelligence is to think that it is simply about getting a cognitive grasp of the concept. While that is useful, what will be of most use to your learners will be your emotionally intelligent approach, not your ability to write a 3000-word critique of the concept. Cognitive learning alone will not do.

Carl Rogers (1902–87) wrote about what would now be called emotional intelligence in teachers, most notably in *Freedom to Learn* (1983). He said that the teacher who exhibited the personal qualities of genuineness, empathy and acceptance with learners would bring about, by that fact alone, change in their learners. (There is more on this in Chapter 7.) However, he was wary of focusing just on skills development in the teacher, which did not change them as a person. He wrote, 'none of the *methods* mentioned in this chapter will be effective unless the teacher's genuine desire is to create a climate in which there is freedom to learn' (Rogers 1983: 157, emphasis in original). He saw procedures and techniques as less important than attitudes. On the other hand, I have seen teachers begin to experiment with changes in their behaviour, which has led to changes in the way they view themselves and others, including their learners. For example, if you experiment with being a more effective listener through active listening skills (see Chapter 7), and if you engage openly in a structured process of reflection on your experiences, this can give you new information about yourself and your view of others and pave the way for you to change that view. The question of how attitude change and skills development relate to each other may be open to debate, but both can be tackled in the process of developing emotional intelligence. There is the opportunity to sample both forms of development through the activities in this book.

Another important consideration when embarking on this kind of development is to remember that it cannot be confined to your role as a teacher. If, for example, you start to be more attentive to your learners, you will find that you will carry this changed behaviour into your other social contexts.

The remainder of this chapter provides four activities for you, designed to assist you in clarifying the concept of using emotional intelligence in your teaching and in beginning to explore how far you already do so.

Activity 1.1

The qualities of an emotionally intelligent teacher

This activity invites you to categorize the different types of quality that good teachers have and to identify the particular qualities associated with teachers who use emotional intelligence.

1. Think of a good teacher whom you have encountered in any context when you were a learner.

2. What words and phrases capture what was good about them?

3. Here are some more words and phrases that are often used to describe good teachers.

Column 1	Column 2	Column 3
Expert	Well-organized	Approachable
Knowledgeable	Manages time well	Acceptant
Authoritative	Useful feedback	Positive
Resourceful	Well prepared	Good listener
Experienced	Good use of materials and teaching aids	Demonstrates empathy
Up-to-date	Clear speaking	Makes eye contact
Can answer any question on the topic	Clear directions	Responsive
	Relevant, interesting and challenging activities	Attentive
	Good materials	Non-threatening
		Open
		Respectful
		Recognizes me
		Doesn't make assumptions

- Words and phrases in the first column relate to the teacher's expertise and subject knowledge.
- Words and phrases in the second column relate to their skills as a teacher.
- Words and phrases in the third column relate to their emotional intelligence.

4. Which words and phrases from the lists above would people apply to you as a teacher? What proportion of these are emotionally intelligent attributes?

Activity 1.2

Providing evidence of the use of emotional intelligence

This activity asks you to find examples from your own experience, both as a learner and as a teacher, of the use of emotional intelligence.

Look over the attributes of a good teacher in column 3 in Activity 1.1 to help you think of the most emotionally intelligent teacher you have ever encountered.

Imagine that this teacher is applying for a post and you have been asked to supply a reference. You know that the interviewers lay great store by the use of emotional intelligence and, indeed, they require you to provide five explicit examples that testify to the candidate's use of emotional intelligence.

What five examples would you choose?

If you were asked to produce evidence of your own use of emotional intelligence, are there five examples that you could cite?

Activity 1.3

Planning for the feelings you wish to generate in your learners

This activity focuses on the teacher's planning for a session. It is good practice in planning for a session to determine learning outcomes that describe what the learners should have achieved by the end of the session. These outcomes ideally should be the basis for determining what the teacher will say and do in the session, what learners will be doing, and what materials will be required and how they will be used. What can be overlooked in planning is thinking about the feelings that learners will hopefully experience. The best conventional session plan might not succeed if it does not take account of how the learners might respond. If, for instance, you are keen that your group will feel curious, or reassured, or resourceful during the session, ask whether the plan as it stands is likely to engender that feeling. If not, consider how to modify the plan to achieve not just the cognitive learning outcomes, but also the emotional responses that will make learning more likely. Remember, the learner who feels:

- **safe** will be more likely to try things out
- **curious** will be more likely to ask questions
- **resourceful** will be more likely to tackle problems
- **motivated** will be more likely to join in
- **inspired** will be more likely to do follow-up work.

1. Choose three feelings from the list below that you particularly want to encourage in your learners.

absorbed	capable	challenged
confident	curious	empowered
encouraged	energized	engaged
enthusiastic	inspired	interested
intrigued	motivated	optimistic
receptive	resourceful	safe
stimulated	understood	valued

2. What do you currently do in your teaching that is likely to encourage these feelings? Be as specific as you can.

3. Are there any ways in which you could you do more to encourage these feelings?

The list of 21 feelings above and the requirement to choose three is arbitrary but the point is to encourage you to think about setting and achieving affective as well as cognitive goals.

Activity 1.4

Being present

Of course, you are physically present when you are there in a room with a group of learners. But the question to ask is, 'Am I wholly here?' You may have taught this session many times before; it's possible you have been with the group before; you may even be very familiar with the room you are in, but remember, this time is different. Being present means being 'in the moment', alert to how things are going and to the responses and mood of the group. It also means that you are ready to respond appropriately to the unexpected. Being present is a prerequisite for all of the behaviours which display emotional intelligence. If you want real communication with your learners, you have to be in the moment with them and not in any way thinking that this is a repeat. This activity provides the chance to review the extent to which you are present with your learners.

Complete the following questionnaire about yourself when teaching.

A = Never B = Rarely C = Sometimes D = Often E = Always					
	A	**B**	**C**	**D**	**E**
1. What I do and say is as much determined by what the learners do and say as by what I have planned	□	□	□	□	□
2. I find myself choosing the best word there and then, rather than sticking to a script	□	□	□	□	□
3. I am ready to show that I have learnt during the session	□	□	□	□	□
4. I am ready to show that I have changed my mind	□	□	□	□	□
5. I am ready to talk with learners about how the session is going	□	□	□	□	□
6. I recognize that I cannot know for sure how the material will be received	□	□	□	□	□
7. I anticipate that I will hear questions and comments that I have never heard before	□	□	□	□	□
8. I negotiate with learners some of the timings in the programme	□	□	□	□	□
9. I negotiate with learners some of the content of the programme	□	□	□	□	□
10. I have some material prepared that I may not use	□	□	□	□	□

The more you are in agreement with these, the more present you are. To develop your readiness to 'be present', just take one of your 'never', 'rarely' or 'sometimes' statements and consider how you could be ready to do more of this in a specific session that's coming up.

Chapter 2

How you relate to your learners

This chapter includes the following activities:

2.1 How do you relate to your learners?
2.2 What's on your T-shirt?
2.3 Your personal style
2.4 Where do you want to get to with your learners?

What does it mean and why does it matter?

A well-developed self-awareness is the first step in being emotionally intelligent (and there is much more on self-awareness in Chapters 10–12). In the context of teaching, before you consider using emotionally intelligent strategies, it is especially important to be aware of how you tend to *relate* to groups of learners. This is because the way in which you relate to your learners will:

- have an immediate effect on how they feel about being in the session – it will affect the emotional environment (see more on this in Chapter 3);
- influence your learners' perception of how they should behave in the session and of the roles available to them;
- set the parameters for your own use of emotional intelligence.

I know that each group is different and always contains a collection of diverse individuals, but it is hard as a teacher not to have an initial view on how to relate to a group. Perhaps you see yourself as the spark to ignite the flame of enquiry in your learners? Or do you see them as potential persecutors who will reveal the inadequacy of your knowledge? Or maybe just as fellow learners who will join you in a journey of discovery? Whichever is the view that you bring to a new group, that view will be at least partially self-fulfilling. Have you ever experienced a colleague who always assumes the worst of a group before meeting them, in terms of their laziness or lack of enthusiasm and so forth? That colleague sees their own role in terms of being a disciplinarian, forcing material on a reluctant audience, perhaps even engaging in crowd control. If their behaviour with the group is based on those expectations, they are more likely to have those expectations confirmed.

Activity 2.1 gives some examples of metaphors that you might use to express how you relate to groups. One example is 'carer to the vulnerable'. If this describes your outlook on learners, they are likely to feel cared for, but there is a danger that your well-intentioned approach may also be cultivating a feeling of dependency in them. Your view of them will affect how they feel. Even if you insist that you are 'neutral' in how you think about them and that you concentrate on your content, methods and materials, that in itself will have an effect. You cannot fail to communicate to your learners your assumptions about your respective roles, and in so doing you will affect how they feel and how they behave.

So, the expectations and the previous experiences of both you and your learners will help shape your relationship. Other factors may also have an influence. If in your teaching you are preparing learners for work in a particular profession or vocation, you may be obliged to reflect the values and behaviours of that profession, for instance, by the way you dress or the way you address each other. Also, constraints on how you and the learners relate to each other may come from the power relationship between you such as when you are ultimately responsible for assessing your learners by determining their grades.

What you need to do is to explore how far you can go in transcending such constraints and to work towards an emotionally healthy relationship with your learners. In particular, if you can achieve a relationship of trust, it can then affect all activities in the classroom. It will affect how your learners behave, how they view you and how they respond to the material. An incidental benefit is that it will allow you to be more flexible in your approach. If you want to experiment with a new activity or method of teaching, your learners are more likely to go along with you when they know that you have their best interests at heart and that they can trust you.

The following section, 'Investigating your practice', has four activities designed to help you explore how far you are aware of how you relate to groups of learners and whether you should work to adopt a more useful view of them. Activities 2.1 and 2.2 invite you to use metaphors and phrases to capture your view of groups of learners. Activities 2.3 and 2.4 draw on Transactional Analysis (TA). TA is a theory of personality and social interaction as well as a tool used in therapy, which has its origins in the 1950s and the work of Eric Berne (1910–70). *TA Today* by Ian Stewart and Vann Joines (1987) remains an excellent introduction to the subject. Julie Hay is also an author on TA whose books give a wealth of everyday applications of the theory. Her *Transactional Analysis for Trainers* (2009) is especially relevant to the focus of this book, whether your work is in training or education. There are other TA-related activities later in this book, namely 9.3, 10.1 and 10.4.

Investigating your practice

Activity 2.1

How do you relate to your learners?

Metaphors are a useful device for standing back from the work you do and capturing it in a phrase that then makes it easier to examine your behaviours and assumptions.

Here are some metaphors for how you might see yourself in relation to a group of your learners:

*   law enforcer to the potentially criminal;
*   carer to the vulnerable;
*   advocate to the jury;
*   salesperson to potential buyers;
*   beekeeper to beehive;
*   sheepdog to sheep;
*   website to surfers;
*   guru to followers;
*   gardener to plants;
*   tour guide to occupants of a tour bus;
*   explorer to fellow explorers.

1. Choose the metaphor that is the best fit for you as a teacher most of the time. You may want to make up a metaphor of your own which fits better.

2. What are the qualities and typical attitude you associate with the role you have chosen for yourself?

3.   What feelings is your adoption of this role likely to trigger in your learners, i.e. what does it feel like to be treated as a prospective buyer, or a sheep or a plant and so on?

4.   Consider your answer to the last question. Are these the feelings you want to encourage in your learners? Are they the best for assisting learning?

Activity 2.2

What's on your T-shirt?

As in Activity 2.1, this is a way of confirming what your message is to your learners and then reflecting on the kind of emotional response this message might provoke in them.

Imagine you are in front of your group of learners wearing a T-shirt. The T-shirt carries a message that tells the group what you are going to do for them. Here are some examples of messages:

I'm gonna show you how much I care

I'm gonna dazzle you with my knowledge

I'm gonna make you laugh and make you think

I'm gonna rescue you

I'm gonna convert you

I'm gonna bring you into line

I'm gonna take you out of your comfort zone

I'm gonna give you whatever you ask for

I'm just gonna be nice to you

1. Take a moment to consider what your message(s) would be. It may be from the list above or you may have a more suitable one of your own.

2. How do you think that your message(s) will make your learners feel? (for example: relieved, frightened, excited, pressured)

3. How will that feeling affect how they relate to you?

4.   How far is their likely response helpful to their learning?

Activity 2.3

Your personal style

A 'personal style' is the term used by Julie Hay (Hay 2009: 75) for an 'ego-state', part of the theory of Transactional Analysis (TA) created by Eric Berne. A personal style describes how you are thinking, feeling and behaving at any one moment. There are three broad categories of personal style: *Parent*, *Adult* and *Child*. When you adopt the *Parent* personal style, you are thinking, feeling and behaving in ways you associate with being a parent, which you absorbed in your very early years from those who were responsible for your upbringing.

When you are using the *Child* personal style, you are replaying the thoughts, feelings and behaviours you recall from the years when you were a young child. When you adopt the personal style of *Adult*, your thoughts, feelings and behaviours are based on what is happening here and now, rather than on your experiences of long ago.

There are two subdivisions of each of the personal styles *Parent* and *Child*: *Controlling Parent* and *Nurturing Parent* and *Natural Child* and *Adapted Child*.

Here are the characteristics of each of the five personal styles and examples of the kinds of thing you might say as a teacher in each style:

Controlling Parent – *directing, firm*
>   'Get into groups'
>   'I am going to stop you here because we must get on to the next activity'

Nurturing Parent – *caring, reassuring*
>   'Don't worry if you can't finish this'
>   'Would you like me to explain that again?'

Adult – *problem-solving, logical*
>   'That is an interesting question'
>   'How do you think we should approach this problem?'

Natural Child – *spontaneous, creative, fun-loving*
    'Let's have some fun with this exercise'
    'I am really excited about what you have just said'

Adapted Child – *compliant and polite OR rebellious and sulking*
    'Is it OK to open the windows?'
    'I would be very grateful if you could fill in this form before you leave'

(The key to *Adapted Child* behaviour is that it is always in response to parental expectations.)

To find out more about your use of personal styles as a teacher, complete the questionnaire on the following page. Each statement relates to you and your learners during a teaching session.

Your use of personal styles is clearly significant in considering how you relate to groups of learners. The point of becoming aware of your personal style preferences is to move from inhabiting them unconsciously to taking more control of them. TA suggests that the reason we are in a particular style at any one time may be because we feel comfortable with that style, because it confirms the view of the world we developed as a young child. Or it may be as a result of a *transaction* with someone else where their behaviour has triggered us to switch to a complementary personal style. For instance, a learner's sulky, non-compliant behaviour (*Adapted Child*) might provoke a teacher, unconsciously, to flip into *Controlling Parent* in an attempt to exert authority over the learner.

It is useful to be aware of your personal style preferences and then to work on adapting your personal style to suit the circumstances. All of them may be employed by a teacher, and the key to using them effectively is to be able to switch personal styles as appropriate. It is also important to recognize and handle others' personal styles. You need to review how balanced your use of personal styles is and to be wary of being driven internally to adopt, for example, *Nurturing Parent* when circumstances suggest it would be more appropriate to adopt, say, *Adult*. Equally, look out for whether the behaviours of learners provoke you into a particular personal style as in the example above. There is more on the transactions between personal styles in Activity 9.3.

For each statement, score as follows:

not true for me	0
partially true for me	1
substantially true for me	2
completely true for me	3

Statement   **Score**

1. I consider my responses to any questions or comments from learners very carefully.

2. I make myself available to offer help to any individuals who have problems.

3. I dress as I imagine learners would expect me to.

4. I make a point of welcoming individuals as they arrive.

5. I am very much 'present' when teaching, in the here-and-now.

6. I deal firmly with learners who cause problems.

7. If a problem arises, I am careful not to rush to a solution.

8. I go to great lengths to reassure learners during a session.

9. For any group activity, I give full and clear details about the task, the time allocation and the outcomes.

10. I make sure there is always some humour in my session.

11. I offer follow-up support to all.

12. I recognize every session is unique and that I must not make assumptions about how things will go.

13. I am respectful of learners' experience.

14. I stick to the schedule.

15. I always look for something new to try in a session.

16. I am always polite and courteous.

17. I am keen that learners enjoy themselves.

18. I do not allow deviations from the topic.

19. I feel I am very open with my learners.

20. I look to agree any changes to the programme with the learners.

Scoring
Put your score for each statement against the number of that statement in the columns below.

	Controlling Parent	Nurturing Parent	Adult	Natural Child	Adapted Child
	6	2	1	10	3
	9	4	5	15	13
	14	8	7	17	16
	18	11	12	19	20
Total					

Now create a bar chart from your scores.

Score					
12					
11					
10					
9					
8					
7					
6					
5					
4					
3					
2					
1					
0					
	Controlling Parent	Nurturing Parent	Adult	Natural Child	Adapted Child

Activity 2.4

Where do you want to get to with your learners?

The concept of 'life positions' is another part of the theory of TA. A life position is a broad view you adopt of yourself in relation to the rest of the world. There are four life positions:

- 'I'm OK, you're OK';
- 'I'm OK, you're not OK';
- 'I'm not OK, you're OK';
- 'I'm not OK, you're not OK'.

This activity uses an alternative set of characterizations of the four life positions:

- 'Get-on-with'; ('I'm OK, you're OK')
- 'Get-rid-of'; ('I'm OK, you're not OK')
- 'Get-away-from'; ('I'm not OK, you're OK')
- 'Get-nowhere-with' ('I'm not OK, you're not OK').

(Stewart and Joines 1987: 119–22)

The key points about life positions are that:

- your preference for one of these will determine how you view incidents and situations. Two people may witness the same behaviour or incident but will interpret it differently because they have different life positions;
- you can change your life position.

Here is an example of how your life position may affect your view of learners.
   A learner says:

> 'I still don't see where this fits into the module.'
> *Get-on-with* sees this as an interesting comment that may be used to expand on the session content.
> *Get-rid-of* sees this as another example of the learner's inadequate grasp of the material.
> *Get-away-from* sees this as a threat to their authority and feels they can only give an inadequate answer.
> *Get-nowhere-with* sees it as just another indication of the futility of the whole session – 'they don't understand and I'm inadequate'.

The questionnaire on the following page helps you to check how your life position may be influencing your view of your learners. For each statement below, think of yourself in relation to the groups you teach or, if they are too diverse, focus on one particular group you know or remember. Indicate whether on the whole you agree or disagree with each statement.

Interpretation

Agreement with any or all of statements 2, 6, 9 and 13 indicates you spend some time in the *get-rid-of* position. This corresponds to the life position '*I'm OK, you're not OK*', a defensive position where you generally see yourself as blameless but are good at seeing failings in others.

   Agreement with any or all of statements 3, 8, 11 and 14 indicates you spend some time in the *get-away-from* position. This corresponds to the life position '*I'm not OK, you're OK*', where you see yourself at fault and others as capable and as potential persecutors.

   Agreement with any or all of statements 4, 7, 10 and 16 indicates you spend some time in the *get-nowhere-with* position. This corresponds to the life position '*I'm not OK, you're not OK*', where you have a negative view of yourself and of everyone else and you experience despair.

	A = Agree B = Disagree	A	B
1.	I enjoy establishing a good working relationship with a group.	☐	☐
2.	They often seem just not motivated to join in.	☐	☐
3.	I am always worried I am going to be asked the question that will catch me out.	☐	☐
4.	When teaching I see myself as making the best of a bad situation.	☐	☐
5.	I feel confident and relaxed in my role.	☐	☐
6.	There always seem to be some learners who are simply lazy.	☐	☐
7.	Sometimes I do wonder 'what's the point?'	☐	☐
8.	I do worry I'm going to be 'found out' as not knowing as much as they think.	☐	☐
9.	Often, I don't think the learners appreciate the value of my expertise.	☐	☐
10.	I sense that nothing really changes.	☐	☐
11.	I often feel I have let at least some of the learners down.	☐	☐
12.	When I approach a new session I expect that both the learners and I will enjoy ourselves and learn something useful.	☐	☐
13.	No matter how much effort I put in there will always be some who are just not going to get it.	☐	☐
14.	I am always conscious of some members of the group who look as though they are not getting much from it.	☐	☐
15.	I enjoy responding to the challenges each new session brings.	☐	☐
16.	Sometimes I think they look as despondent as I feel.	☐	☐

Agreement with any or all of statements 1, 5, 12 and 15 indicates you spend some time in the *get-on-with* position. This corresponds to the life position '*I'm OK, you're OK*', described as the only position based on reality, where you are ready to acknowledge situations for how they really are, to be open-minded and to tackle problems.

If any of your answers match positions other than *get-on-with*, take note the next time you experience related feelings with a group. How much is your perception based on reality and how much are you using it to confirm a long-held view of the world? Remember, life positions can be changed but that can demand a significant shift in how you explain yourself, your relationships and your social environment.

Developing your practice

Use your findings from the four activities above as the basis for plans to develop your practice. For example, if you discover that your prevalent metaphor in 2.1 or your preferred T-shirt message in 2.2 is likely to generate feelings in your learners that are not conducive to learning, consider how to move yourself into a more productive view.

Making changes in response to your findings in the TA-related activities above is not always easy. If these patterns of behaviour and attitudes are based on your experience of the world when you were very young and vulnerable, it takes more than a simple cognitive decision to become different. Being aware of your personal style and life position is a first step, and that is what the activities above are designed to achieve. The possible next step is to be attentive to your behaviour, thoughts and feelings and to plan when to try out alternatives.

There is a particular task you can do in relation to activity 2.3. To begin to exert more control over your use of personal styles, look at your bar chart. Consider whether you would like to change the distribution of personal styles on the chart. If there is one that you would like to spend less time in, which one(s) would you like to increase in its place? Plan the kinds of behaviour and phrases you could use to increase the time you spend in this personal style and if you succeed, you will find you spend less time in the undesired style.

Chapter 3

Planning the emotional environment

This chapter includes the following activities:

What does it mean and why does it matter?

Eric Jensen asserts that the state you are in is the most important factor determining your readiness to learn. He writes, 'All learning is state dependent' (Jensen 1998: 192). State is characterized by the collection of emotions you are feeling. In a learning state you experience those feelings that are more conducive to learning, for example valued, curious, safe, relaxed, engaged and motivated. A resourceful state affects the physiological processes of the brain in such a way that learning is more likely. You are ready to put your energies into learning and not into 'non-learning' activities such as disengagement and defensiveness.

Of course, there is a great deal of potential in the classroom situation to induce feelings that do not create a learning state. With a colleague, I surveyed three groups of learners in higher education with questions about their experience of what we termed 'classroom climate' and lecturer qualities.

One question we asked of respondents was to name 'some of the feelings I have come to associate with my favourite session'. Responses to this question included 'enthusiastic', 'fascination', 'happy and alive', 'enjoyment', 'being valued', 'confident', 'curious', 'excited'. With another question we asked for feelings associated with their least favourite session. The most frequently recurring response here was 'boredom', but others included 'annoyed', 'frustration', 'impatient', 'anger', 'excluded', 'depressed', 'alienation', 'resentment', 'humiliated', 'intimidated'. When feelings such as those in the latter list are dominant, the brain switches into what has been characterized as the 'fight or flight' mode and physiological processes are activated which restrict the functions in the brain that assist learning.

The learning state of an individual learner in the classroom will be to some extent shaped by what they bring to the session. This will include their reasons for being there, their previous experience of being a learner, and whatever is uppermost in their thoughts and concerns at the time. The other major contributor to the learning state of learners is the emotional environment – their overall experience of being in the classroom. The emotional environment is shaped by many factors. Important ones include:

- what the teacher says and does;
- what the learners say and do;
- the physical experience of the learners;
- the language that is used by the teacher;
- the materials and how they are used;
- the activities that the learners engage in.

An ideal learning state has been described by Mihalyi Csikszentmihalyi as 'flow' (Csikszentmihalyi 1997). Flow is that state when you are completely absorbed by a task and when there is a balance between your ability and the demands of the task – not so difficult that it creates feelings of helplessness and anxiety, but not so easily achievable that it could result in boredom. In addition there need to be clear goals and structure and no sense of pressure or anxiety that distracts you and prevents absorption. Csikszentmihalyi describes the state of flow as a 'magnet for learning' (ibid.: 33). To encourage flow in your learners, see if you can create activities for them where:

- goals are clear
- feedback is available
- control is experienced
- the task matches the skills
- the reward is in the task
- there is no chance of failure.

You are bound to have an effect, by accident or design, on how your learners feel during a session. While you are not solely responsible for how they feel, your role in influencing the emotional environment and the learning state of your learners is crucial. Most teachers are aware of the concept of emotional environment but perhaps do not consciously put as much energy into affecting it as it deserves. If the emotional environment is wrong, learning will always be a struggle. I suggest you should plan to create a positive emotional environment and, in your planning, give this at least as much attention as the content and your methods.

In the remainder of this chapter, the section *Investigating your practice* begins with five activities designed to help you look critically at how you currently plan for the emotional environment. Activity 3.6 in *Developing your practice* builds on your findings from these five activities. Activities 3.7 and 3.8 suggest other strategies for influencing the emotional environment. Remember, not only should you plan for it, you should monitor it and attempt to adjust it if necessary. It needs vigilance on your part. It is dynamic, not fixed, and any event or comment in the session has the potential to instantly affect the environment.

A useful question to ask yourself is, 'Am I helping to create an emotional environment in which my learners feel:

- safe rather than threatened?
- trustful rather than suspicious?
- challenged rather than pressured?
- motivated rather than disengaged?
- curious rather than indifferent?
- resourceful rather than powerless?
- enthused rather than bored?
- adventurous rather than defensive?

Investigating your practice

Activity 3.1

Where do you put your planning energy?

This activity asks you to reflect on how much time you spend planning for the use of emotional intelligence compared with planning for content, methods and materials. This is especially important in a first meeting with a group of learners where the tone is set and the basis for the relationship between the teacher and the group is formed.

As a percentage of the energy you spend planning a session, how much goes into planning content?

As a percentage of the energy you spend planning a session, how much goes into planning methods and materials?

As a percentage of the energy you spend planning a session, how much goes into planning to use emotional intelligence?

Represent these proportions on a pie chart as in this example:

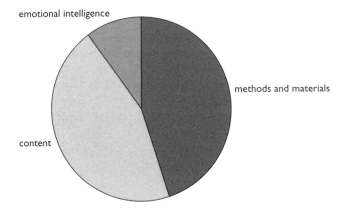

Consider whether this represents your ideal balance between these three components. If you want to devote more energy to planning to use emotional intelligence, activity 3.6 below suggests a way to do this.

Activity 3.2

Your use of language at the start of a session

This activity invites you to review the impact of your opening words. Words can have a profound effect on our state of mind. The words you use with learners can encourage a learning 'state' in them. The language you use at the start of a session may be more important than that used later, as it sets the tone. In particular, the first few minutes can be crucial in shaping the learners' view of you and of the session. This activity asks you how far you want to go in trying to create the right state in your learners.

Here are three examples of the use of language at the start of a session.

Dull

Hello everyone. Welcome to the course. We have got a lot to get through today; some of it I suspect you'll find less interesting than other parts. Unfortunately, there will not be much time for questions, but at least I can give you handouts to take away.

Positive

I am excited at the prospect of going through this material with you – I have used it with a range of groups who have all been very positive in their responses. I am sure that you will find plenty of relevance and use in today's session and my plan is to make it enjoyable as well as interesting.

Over-the-top

I am genuinely thrilled to be doing this with you today. What I am going to tell you today is some of the most valuable information you have ever heard. As you can see, I have even arranged for a sunny day. Personally I can't wait to get going!

1. Think of a session that you have run recently.
2. Word a positive introduction – in your own style.
3. Now word an over-the-top introduction – with words that you might even consider using.

Here are examples of positive words and phrases you might use:

fantastic	joy	better	I promise
enjoy	energy	excited	I guarantee
adventure	elated	satisfy	I welcome
thrilled	certain	I will definitely	I am convinced

Activity 3.3

Handouts

The use of handouts may be declining as materials become more readily available online, but a handout can still be a key component of many teaching sessions, especially when they are used in for learning activities. What you see influences how you feel. How many times have you witnessed learners on a course complain about a handout – because it is poorly copied or typed, there is too much to take in, the type is too small and so on? This activity gives you the opportunity to review a handout from that perspective.

Find a handout, preferably one that you have been given but otherwise one that you have used yourself.

Comment critically on each item from the following checklist:

the font Including, what feelings word would you use for the font? e.g. stern; friendly; authoritative; boring	
the number of words Are these sufficient? Can they be instantly digested?	
the size of the type Including, is it too small/too large? Is it/should it be the same throughout?	
any pictures or diagrams Are there too many/too few? How clear are they?	
the use of bold and italics Is it too often, too infrequent?	
the colour of the paper Would the handout be better on another colour?	
overall layout Is it welcoming or off-putting?	

How would you describe the handout overall?
    For example, *sparse; messy; cluttered; well laid out*

How does the look of the handout make you feel?

For example, *impressed; dispirited; irritated; reassured; inspired*

As a result of your responses, draft a new improved version of a part of the handout.

Please note, to maximize its accessibility, a handout should:

have a sans serif font, for example Arial, Trebuchet, Verdana;
be no less than 12 point;
avoid excessive underlining, capitals and italics;
have good contrast between the font colour and the background colour;
be left-aligned, not justified;
be not too dense, avoiding long blocks of continuous text, making use of bullet points and lists where suitable;
use wide margins and spaces between paragraphs.

Activity 3.4

Maintaining variety of experience for your learners

The brain needs a variety of stimuli to work at its best. Too much of any one stimulus, however good in itself, can lead to feelings of boredom, withdrawal or frustration. This activity invites you to review how much variety is experienced by your learners.

Consider the last session you ran.

Note how many minutes were spent on each of these activities:

1. You talking to the group _____
2. You showing PowerPoint slides _____
3. You writing on a flipchart _____
4. You writing on a whiteboard _____
5. You showing things to the group _____

6. You demonstrating to the group_____

7. Dialogue between you and the group_____

8. Learners solving problems_____

9. Learners engaging in discussion_____

10. Learners answering questions_____

11. Learners trying out a procedure or practical activity_____

12. Learners analysing a case study_____

13. Learners planning to test theories_____

14. Other activities_____

Do you think the balance of these activities is satisfactory? Be wary of saying that a good mix of numbers 1 to 6 is balanced for the learners, as you are expecting similar behaviour from them in each instance – passive, perhaps taking notes, with perhaps a minority asking questions.

Activity 3.5

Accommodating your learners' differing intelligences

Howard Gardner introduced the concept of Multiple Intelligences in his 1983 book, *Frames of Mind*, and has continued to refine it since, for example in *Multiple Intelligences* (Gardner 2006). He rejects the question, 'How intelligent are you?' in favour of 'How are you intelligent?' He suggests that we have differing intelligence profiles, based on the extent to which we have developed our potential in each of our intelligences. He originally identified seven intelligences. They are: linguistic, logical-mathematical, spatial, bodily-kinaesthetic, musical, interpersonal, and intrapersonal.

Gardner's ideas have been criticized, most notably by John White, who questions the foundations on which the concept is based, whilst acknowledging that it has proved useful to some educators (White 2004). However, it may be that the way a learner feels in a session can be influenced by the extent to which their dominant intelligence (or preferred style of learning) is catered for. This activity suggests how you could prevent any learners from feeling excluded in this way.

Here are the types of learning activity likely to suit each intelligence:

Linguistic

Likely to respond well to learning activities such as those which involve:
- a variety of text and auditory stimulus; the chance to talk through new concepts; giving a talk; creative writing; verbal debate.

Logical-mathematical

Likely to respond well to learning activities such as those which involve:
- using abstract symbols to represent concrete objects and concepts; seeing patterns in ideas and relationships; solving logical puzzles and working out sequences; cause-and-effect analysis; calculating; estimating.

Spatial

Likely to respond well to learning activities such as those which involve:
- imagining; drawing; designing; construction; painting; Mind-Mapping.

Bodily/kinaesthetic

Likely to respond well to learning activities such as those which involve:
- movement, touch or other physical experiences; hands-on projects; role-play; working with objects.

Musical

Likely to respond well to learning activities such as those which involve:
- using rhymes, songs or other rhythmical patterns to aid memory.

Interpersonal

Likely to respond well to learning activities such as those which involve:
- cooperative learning; considering issues from a range of perspectives; interpersonal problem-solving; giving feedback; receiving feedback; active listening.

Intrapersonal

Likely to respond well to learning activities such as those which involve:
- time for reflection; self-assessment; feelings responses; developing self-awareness.

Is there one or more of these intelligences and learning activity preferences that describes you?

We often teach in the way that we like to learn and we respond best to learners who learn in the same way as we do. However, if your teaching does not include activities for all preferences, some individuals will have less of a sense of belonging and may feel excluded.

Take each intelligence in turn and, looking back on a recent session, ask yourself what you did to connect with learners who would prefer to use that intelligence.

Type of Intelligence	What did I do to connect?
Linguistic	
Logical-mathematical	
Spatial	
Bodily/kinaesthetic	

Musical	
Interpersonal	
Intrapersonal	

DEVELOPING YOUR PRACTICE

Activity 3.6

Planning for meeting a new group

Planning to use emotional intelligence is particularly important when you are meeting a new group of learners. This activity suggests five key areas to consider in planning and scheduling activities that help to create a positive emotional environment for a new group. All but the second one should be suitable with groups of any size.

I will ensure everyone gets to speak in the first _ minutes.
How?

(this helps individuals feel part of the group, as long as what they have to say is not too threatening or awkward for them.)

· I will have used everyone's name in the first _ minutes.
How?

(See Chapter 6)

I will have dealt with some potential anxieties in the first _ minutes.
How?

(See Chapter 5)

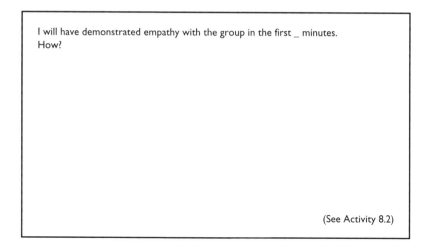

I will have demonstrated empathy with the group in the first _ minutes.
How?

(See Activity 8.2)

I will have revealed something personal about myself in the first _ minutes.
How?

(See Chapter 14)

Activity 3.7

Finding out about your learners as individuals

This activity looks at how you can introduce personal information about the learners into the session, while keeping the session relevant to the topic in hand. Such information can affect the environment for the better because it reminds everyone that, behind the role of learner, there are people too. Depending on the topic, it can also produce a great deal of humour!

Think of a course that you run, and then choose a specific topic that is included on the course. Create a question that could be asked of all members of the group that could provide a focus for them in understanding the topic and at the same time reveal something about them as individuals. A number of individual answers could be heard by the group as a whole. This can work with groups of up to about 40.

Look at the examples below. Then create some questions of your own.

Example 1

On a course about how people learn, there is an activity that begins by asking learners to think of one thing they are good at. The point of this brief activity is to explore how they became good at whatever it is and, from that starting point, to consider what makes for effective learning. Before asking the follow-up questions, you can ask everyone in turn to state the thing they have identified themselves as good at.

This reveals positive personal information about everyone to the whole of the group and it can have a very beneficial effect on the environment. Learners will have had the chance to declare something personal about themselves that is not necessarily connected with why they are there. It is also a positive aspect of themselves that they have revealed. This activity can have the same effect as an icebreaker but be directly integrated into a session.

Example 2

A teacher is introducing the topic of information retrieval. The teacher asks each person in the group to say what system they use (if any) at home for storing things, e.g. CDs, bills, tools, books.

Activity 3.8

Developing emotional intelligence through learner activities

One important factor that has an effect on the emotional environment in the classroom is learners' behaviour. You can encourage more emotionally intelligent behaviours on the part of learners by introducing learning activities which, in themselves, invite the learners to behave in emotionally intelligent ways.

Here are three such activities.

Five minutes each way

- Learners are in pairs.
- One talks (with the focus as directed by you, e.g. 'what I have learnt from today's session so far'), the other listens.
- The listener is attentive and mostly silent, not starting to talk about themselves and not taking the talker off course.
- The talker has the chance to articulate their thoughts, responses or feelings about the course so far.
- After five minutes they swap roles.

This could be used at any point in the session. When used at the beginning, it can act as an icebreaker, with learners talking about, for example, what they already know about the topic. The method may also be used in the middle or at the end of the session, with learners using the five minutes for making sense of the session, for recalling content, for making plans to use the content, or for beginning to reflect on the content. The listener can learn a great deal through the discipline of being attentive and putting themselves into the speakers' frame of reference (see Activity 7.3).

Giving feedback

On courses where participants have been learning a skill, create the chance for one to perform a skill (learner A) and for another to observe the performance (learner B). Guide B in the principles of giving effective feedback, which include:

- start with the positive comments
- follow the initial positive comments with any comments that are more critical and be sure to end with positive comments
- confine any critical feedback to the amount the recipient can handle rather than the amount you would like to give
- make sure the feedback is something the recipient is in a position to act on
- make observations, not inferences
- be specific rather than generalizing
- use a supportive tone of voice.

Direct B to give feedback to A on A's performance, guided by these principles. This activity forces B to consider A's perspective both when planning feedback and when giving feedback.

Action learning sets

For courses that involve the same group meeting on more than one occasion, with intervals in between, it may be appropriate to arrange for the learners to use action learning sets. If, for example, your sessions are a day long, you could set aside 60–90 minutes of the day for learners to meet in action learning sets. An action learning set normally has four or five members. Each meeting of the set gives each member an equal amount of time to draw on the help of the other members to solve their problem and/or to progress with their development. Prepare the group members by explaining the key points in the process and their roles.

Key points in the process:

- Keep the focus on the 'presenter' – the member who is the focus for that period of time
- Other group members listen, support, challenge
- Maintain an equal distribution of time
- Maintain a cooperative and positive atmosphere
- Ensure clear action planning by the presenter at the end of their time, for example 'what I must do before we meet again'.

Roles:

Each set must have one of each of these:

- chair/time-keeper
- note-taker – keeps a record of the outcomes of each member's allocated time
- reporter – reports to the rest of the group at the end of the meeting on how far the group stuck to the key points in the process.

Stress that it is essential for the group to save time at the end of a meeting to hear from the reporter and to review how well they operated as a set.

Liz Beaty and Ian McGill have noted that 'Learning to use empathy within a set can be one of the most important developmental experiences from the action learning process itself' (Beaty and McGill 2001: 26). Their book, *Action Learning*, gives detailed information on the operation of action learning sets.

Chapter 4

Planning for the physical experience of learners

This chapter includes the following activities:

4.1 What is the physical experience of your learners?
4.2 Shaping your learners' physical experience
4.3 Ensuring that your learners get moving

What does it mean and why does it matter?

It is easy to overlook the physical experience of your learners when you are planning for a session, and yet our physical experience is entwined with our emotional experience. This means that the teacher who wishes to create positive emotional states in their learners has to consider what is going to happen to those learners physically in the session.

Candace Pert, in her book *Molecules of Emotion*, asserts that the areas of study for each of three separate disciplines – neuroscience, endocrinology and immunology – are in fact linked. The link is neuropeptides, which she dubs 'information carriers'. As a result, 'every change in the physiological state is accompanied by an appropriate change in the mental emotional state, conscious or unconscious' (Pert 1999: 137). This feels intuitively right – your physical state affects your emotional state – but it becomes very significant for teachers if we accept Pert's suggestion that we should think of the 'mobile brain' within our bodies. This is the term she uses for the 'psychosomatic network through which intelligent information travels from one system to another' (ibid.: 188).

This view is endorsed from the perspective of neuroscience by Antonio Damasio. He speaks of the body and the brain being an 'indissociable organism' (Damasio 1996: xviii). You cannot fully understand mental processes unless you take into account the context in which they are operating, that is, how the organism of the body and brain interacts with the physical and social environment. Most importantly, 'feeling depends on activity in a number of specific brain systems interacting with a number of body organs' (ibid.: xviii). The learner's brain that you are trying to connect with as you teach may be located in the head, but it is fully integrated with the rest of the body. The physical, emotional and learning states are interlinked. This means that if you want to influence your learners' readiness to learn, you have to address the whole person, including what happens to them physically during the session.

It is useful to consider three components of the learners' physical experience when planning:

- movement;
- the physical environment;
- comfort.

Movement

Even though it is known that sitting down for long periods of time does not help learning, there is a tradition in most areas of education and training that the learners sit down and stay seated for the duration of the session. Have you ever been aware that one or more of your learners has begun to nod off? Perhaps you thought it was because you were boring or because the person was not fit and alert themselves. Have you ever considered it is simply because they have had no chance to move? While you have been distributing handouts, moving to and from the flipchart or whiteboard or laptop, talking and generally being quite physically active, they have been immobile and mostly silent. The minimum you can do is to ensure that they are standing for at least some of the time, which will lead to an increase in the amount of oxygenated blood going to the brain. This in turn arouses the nervous system and leads to neural firing and the growth of the dendrites and axons that make the connections that lead to learning.

The physical environment

Have you ever considered what learners can see when they are in a session? In the traditional classroom arrangement, most learners will have a good view of the backs of other learners' heads. They may also be in one of those rooms that look like they were designed, if that is the right word, for interrogation or imprisonment, so stark and bare is the environment. This could well be another effect of the Cartesian assumption that learning is solely about a meeting of minds (see pages 4–5). This view holds that the intellect alone is active when learning takes place and, as it is separate from body and soul, the environment is irrelevant. Even when you are in a reasonable room you may find that it has been used by others for what might politely be called 'storage' or, more accurately, 'dumping'. You may be faced with spare furniture, boxes and so on that are at best a distraction and at worst a subliminal depressing influence on the room's inhabitants. All of these factors affect your learners' disposition towards the session. Underestimate them and your carefully planned session will lose some of its impact. The least you can do is create time to make the environment inoffensive, with nothing unsightly. If you are able, take the time to arrange the seating and introduce peripherals such as posters or relevant, rolling screensavers or music at break times, to improve this aspect of the learners' physical experience.

Comfort

The suitability of the seating, lighting and heating is not always within your control but you can investigate just how far you can make changes. Those feedback forms which say, 'great session but the chairs were very uncomfortable' are not flippant and you should be ready to check your learners' level of comfort during the session.

Activity 4.1 asks you to appreciate the perspective of learners in terms of their physical experience in a session and to explore possible improvements. Activities 4.2 and 4.3 invite you to consider ways of improving your learners' physical experience of your sessions.

Investigating your practice

Activity 4.1

What is the physical experience of your learners?

Look at the checklist below. Take a session that you have run recently, preferably in a room with which you are familiar. For each physical factor, answer the three questions.

Physical factor	What normally happens?	How much control do I have over this?	How could I change it for the better?
1. Where the learners sit			
2. How long the learners sit			
3. Whether the learners have the opportunity to move			

Continued on next page

Physical factor	What normally happens?	How much control do I have over this?	How could I change it for the better?
4. If they do have the opportunity to move, in what way and how often?			
5. What your learners see			
6. The learners' proximity to each other			
7. The lighting			
8. The temperature			
9. The contents of the room			
10. Any other physical factors in the environment			

Developing your practice

Activity 4.2

Shaping your learners' physical experience

Look at your entries in column four, in activity 4.1, 'How could I change it for the better?'

Take each of your responses in that column in turn and plan how to introduce those changes for a forthcoming session. Consider whether you need to:

- speak to anybody about moving to another room or changing the furniture or contents of the room around;
- acquire anything to add to the environment such as posters, music;
- integrate learner movement into your session plan;
- negotiate any aspect of their physical experience with your learners.

Activity 4.3

Ensuring that your learners get moving

Here are six suggestions that will ensure that your learners do more than just sit. Remember with all of these to say to the learners that if mobility or standing is difficult for anyone, they may of course stay seated.

1. When learners are forming groups for small-group work, ask them to get together with one or two others who are 'not sitting next to you' or 'not from your table' or 'from the opposite side of the room' or 'whom you have not worked with or spoken to yet in the session'.

2. If you use handouts, instead of distributing them, place them in piles around the room and ask everyone to collect one.

3. Ask participants to stand while carrying out any brief activity in twos or threes.

4. Ask participants to 'promenade', i.e. walk and talk with each other while carrying out any brief activity in pairs.

5. Arrange a 'line-up' – learners are asked to stand in one line. Their place in the line is determined by where they 'stand' on a statement that relates to the topic of the session, for example:
    Managers spend too much time focusing on the endpoint of the change, not the transition.

The line stretches from 'wholly agree' to 'wholly disagree'.

(The point of such an activity, apart from stimulating movement, is to encourage learners to consider their opinion on a topic and, in order to get to the right point in the line, they are forced to speak with others to find out their position, thereby engaging with each other and with the topic.)

6. Consider taking five-minute breaks more frequently.

Chapter 5

Dealing with your learners' expectations

This chapter includes the following activities:

5.1 Addressing learners' fears
5.2 Passing on the information, part one
5.3 Passing on the information, part two
5.4 Ground rules
5.5 Hopes and expectations, fears and worries
5.6 Exchanging expectations
5.7 Your way is OK

What does it mean and why does it matter?

When you next meet a group of learners for the first time, take a look at the individuals assembled there. They will include people who feel excited, hopeful, fearful, anxious, vulnerable and impatient. There will be the keen and the curious, the cynical and the defensive. These feelings will be based, for the most part, on their assumptions about the course ahead. They will all have *expectations* about what is going to happen. They are likely to be asking themselves questions such as:

- Will it be death by PowerPoint?
- Will I have to do those embarrassing role-plays?
- Will I have to speak?
- Will we finish on time?
- What if I don't understand?

From your experience, as a teacher or as a learner, I am sure you can think of other kinds of question they might be asking.

If you are concerned about having a positive influence on the emotional state of your learners, it is essential for you to take steps to acknowledge and influence this range of initial feelings. You have to display your emotional intelligence by *dealing with your learners' expectations*.

It is easy, in the role of teacher, to overlook or underestimate the power of these feelings. You may be very familiar with the course you are about to run. You know the material very well and, because you have planned the course, you have a clear picture of what is going to happen when. It is true that you may have anxieties of your own, but do not forget that you will always have the advantage over your learners of knowing in detail what is planned.

Your learners will have expectations based on their previous experience of being in similar situations. They are likely to have expectations which relate to how they will behave, think and feel; to their role as a learner; to the content; and to your role as a teacher. They may well have an initial expectation about how useful the course will be. It is most likely that some individuals within the group will have different expectations from each other and it is very possible that your expectations may differ from some or from the entire group.

If expectations are not dealt with, there is the potential for a great deal of learner energy going into unproductive emotions such as anxiety and frustration. If one of them is sitting there worrying about, for example, whether the session is going to end on time, that is energy diverted away from participating fully in the session. If the expectations of an individual do not match what is going to happen, that could eventually lead to frustration and disappointment on their part when they realize those expectations are not going to be fulfilled.

It is important to deal with expectations because:

- you can prevent learner energy from being wasted on unproductive emotions;
- if you take the time to hear their expectations, you are in a better position to make connections between your material and your learners' interests or concerns;
- the very act of acknowledging your learners' hopes, worries and so on has a positive effect on how they feel;
- it initiates a productive relationship between you and your learners, characterized by dialogue and the sharing of information.

Key questions to ask yourself are:

- Should I provide the opportunity for individuals to air their expectations, anxieties and so on?
- How far should I attempt to acknowledge their expectations, anxieties and so on?
- Am I sharing all of the information I have that will be useful to them about what is going to happen?
- Should I arrange for any negotiation about what is going to happen?

Leigh O'Brien, in her article 'Caring in the Ivory Tower' (O'Brien 2010), makes the case for 'deliberately creating and nurturing a caring teacher–student relationship' (ibid.: 110). She writes about how she invited her new class of trainee teachers to meet with her, one-to-one, at the start of the semester, simply to get to know them as individuals. Twenty-four of her 29 learners took up the offer and there were positive comments about the experience in the end-of-semester evaluations. Apart from making a good teacher–student relationship more likely, such a meeting should provide an excellent opportunity to hear about and acknowledge the expectations and hopes and so on of individual learners, making the teacher better prepared to reflect these when the class begins.

The section *Investigating your practice* that follows has three activities that invite you to examine the extent to which you currently deal with expectations. *Developing your practice* has four activities which suggest strategies you can use for dealing with expectations in a new group. Which strategies you use depends on, among other things, the duration of the course and the number of learners you have. Of course, it would be inappropriate to use all of them, because they overlap.

Investigating your practice

Activity 5.1

Addressing learners' fears

Thomas Sappington described four kinds of fear that adult learners typically have when a new class starts (Sappington 1984). They are:

Outcome fears

These include: 'Will it be a waste of time?' 'Will there be enough time to absorb everything?' 'Will I get what I need to know?'

Evaluation fears

These include: 'Will there be a test?' 'Will I fail?'

Interpersonal fears

These relate to exchanges with both the teacher and other learners. They include: 'Will I get clear directions from the teacher?' 'Will I be put on the spot?' 'Is there a potential for embarrassment?'

Internal fears

These include: 'Will I feel inadequate or incompetent?' 'Will I find that I have to change?'

Take each kind of fear in turn and ask, 'What do I currently do to anticipate these fears in my learners and to allay them? Is there more I could do?'

1. **Outcome fears**

2. **Evaluation fears**

3. **Interpersonal fears**

4. **Internal fears**

Activity 5.2

Passing on the information, part one

Consider a session that you have run with a group that was new to you. How and when did you ensure that the following was clear to all learners?

- Your style of teaching
- What your group will be expected to do as learners
- What learners can expect to gain from the session and how this will be achieved
- Why the learners are doing this; for example, how it is related to their work or to their learning needs
- An outline of the content
- Who is expected to speak when and how
- If you will be meeting on a regular basis, what time subsequent sessions will start, in reality
- Times of breaks
- What time sessions finish, in reality
- Whether or not the material you are displaying, such as a PowerPoint presentation or video clips, will be available to the learners in any other way such as online or on a handout.

What other essential information did you have that your learners needed to know?

Activity 5.3

Passing on the information, part two

This is an activity for you if you are involved in assessing your learners. Take an assessed course that you are responsible for. With regard to the assessment, which of the following is known to the learners?

- What skills and knowledge they will be assessed on
- When that assessment will happen
- What form it takes
- How it is marked
- Who marks it
- What the criteria are for success in the assessment
- How the criteria are applied to the task
- How soon after the assessment they will know the result
- How to find out the result
- When and how to regain their work
- Whether feedback is available and, if so, when and how

- How the work they are doing now relates to the assessment
- What guidance they can get in preparing for the assessment.

Are there any other facts relating to the assessment that your learners should know?

Developing your practice

One simple approach to developing your practice is to revisit the checklists in activities 5.2 and 5.3 above. You may recite all the information in 5.2 at the beginning of a session, but it is worth simply asking learners whether there are any questions or comments before you move on. For the information on assessment in 5.3, you might say that all of this is *available* to your learners as it is provided in a course guide. It is worth considering whether you need to do more to ensure that the information is *received and understood* by learners. This could be done by providing regular opportunities for learners to ask about assessment. There is every likelihood that you will find yourself repeating details, but that may be what is needed to ensure that learners are reassured about the process. Lewis Elton suggests that clarity about assessment improves the extrinsic motivation of learners, as they can be clearer about what is required for success (Elton 1996). None of this means that they will be less anxious about passing the assessment, but it removes those anxieties that stem from uncertainty about what is required.

Other options include:

- Establish ground rules, through negotiation or simply by declaring them;
- Arrange for discussion of 'hopes and expectations, fears and worries';
- Exchange with the group your expectations of them and theirs of you;
- Let your learners know that 'their way is OK'.

Each of these four strategies is explained below.

Activity 5.4

Ground rules

Ground rules specify acceptable behaviour for learners on a course. The following three approaches to devising ground rules for a course give learners the chance to take some control over the rules, to collaborate with other learners, and to take account of the needs of other learners. In this way, the process of agreeing rules not only gives clarity about what everyone may expect but also increases motivation and the potential for collaborative learning.

Here are three ways to agree a set of ground rules for the operation of a group. They all assume that the group does not consist of more than 15 people and that this group is going to meet on a regular basis.

Method A

1. Distribute a provisional set of rules such as this sample set.
   Sample set of ground rules
   - We will always begin no later than five minutes after the agreed start time and end no later than the agreed finish time.
   - We will review the scheduled programme at the start of each session to consider whether we need more or less time on any items.
   - Any group member may speak at any time.
   - Anyone who wishes to speak may not interrupt but should indicate they wish to speak by raising their hand.
   - We will ensure that everyone has equal opportunity to speak.
   - Everyone's opinions may be challenged but will be respected.
   - Everything that is discussed in this group is confidential and cannot be repeated outside the group without the speaker's permission.
2. Allow a few minutes for everyone to consider them.
3. Go through each item with the group, in order to:
   - ensure there is a common understanding;
   - invite rewording of it;
   - work on reaching a consensus on whether to adopt it.
4. Receive any suggestions for additional rules and then go through steps 2 and 3 again.
5. Display the agreed set of rules.
6. For subsequent sessions, display the rules again or provide copies of them for everyone.

Method B

1. Display or give a copy of the list below to the group:
   - Who speaks, when and how
   - Interruptions
   - Confidentiality
   - Punctuality
   - Ensuring shared time for speaking
   - Responding to each other's opinions.
2. Discuss each issue in turn to arrive at relevant rules, each of which has to be accepted by the group.
3. Write out the agreed set of rules and display or distribute them.

Method C

1. Ask each person to write down, on separate pieces of paper, any ground rules they would wish for the group.
2. Collect them.

3. Group any similar suggestions together.
4. Take each cluster of suggestions in turn to discuss as a group and attempt to reach a consensus about a rule.
5. Write out the agreed set of rules and display or distribute them.

Activity 5.5

Hopes and expectations, fears and worries

This activity shows how you can spend time at the beginning of a course giving everyone the chance to articulate their hopes, expectations, fears and worries.

Providing this opportunity should, in itself, greatly aid learners' engagement with the course and will signal that these matters are important and that it is appropriate to talk about them. Individuals will also almost certainly see that they are not alone in their fears and worries. They will also get the chance to receive reassurance or guidance from you as a teacher. You may even adjust some aspect of your approach in light of what they say. This process will be another means of developing a productive dialogue between you and your learners.

Step 1

At the start of a session ask individuals to take five minutes to think what are:

*   their hopes and expectations;
*   their fears and worries

about the course and, if they wish, to write them down in two columns.

Step 2

Ask them to find a partner and spend five to ten minutes asking that person about their hopes and expectations, fears and worries.

Step 3

Ask each pair to join with another pair. Give out flipchart paper and marker pens to each group of four. Each person takes it in turn to introduce their partner's list to the other two, making sure that their partner has the chance to modify what is said. Each group of four produces a summary on one side of flipchart paper of their hopes and expectations, fears and worries. This should take 10–15 minutes. During this time, you too have been recording your hopes and expectations, fears and worries on one side of flipchart paper.

Step 4

All flipcharts are displayed.

Step 5

Take five minutes for everyone to look at all of them.

Step 6

You respond to what is written, taking care to:

- acknowledge everything that is written, without judgement;
- provide information as appropriate.

Allow 10–15 minutes.

Activity 5.6

Exchanging expectations

Distribute copies of the list below, 'As a learner, I expect', to your group, or number the items and display them for all to see. Ask the learners to look at the list and decide which of the statements match their expectations.

Then ask for a show of hands on each item, such as, 'How many of you have ticked "to be asked what I want"?' This gives you an indication of the expectations of the group as a whole. You can respond to each item by explaining how far it matches what you are planning. This activity gives you and your learners the chance to explore how far your expectations match. Its benefits are:

- It indicates to you whether you need to consider modifying your plans, if your learners' expectations are so far from yours that they will feel alienated.
- It gives you the chance to show that you acknowledge and respect your learners' expectations, even if you are not going to meet all of them.
- It initiates dialogue between you and your learners.
- Crucially, it lessens the chance for growing frustration on your learners' part should they gradually realize that their expectations are not to be met.

As a learner, I expect:

- to be told what to do
- that the teacher knows more than me
- to be asked what I want
- to influence the progress of the session/course

- to be told whether I am right or wrong
- to be made welcome
- to decide for myself what I want to get out of the session/course
- that the teacher knows what will be covered in a session/course
- to be helped by other learners
- that I will be encouraged to apply the learning to my personal circumstances
- that the knowledge I gain will be from the teacher
- to help other learners learn
- to provide information useful to the teacher
- that I will make notes
- to be asked what I think
- to be asked to evaluate the session/course
- to ensure that I learn something
- the teacher to ensure that I learn something.

You may want to use this additional checklist, 'As a teacher, I expect' to explain the alternatives open to you, which you will be opting for and why.

As a teacher, I expect:

- to make a session plan
- to assess learners
- to respond to the individual needs of learners
- to determine the aims of the session
- learners to assess themselves
- to allow the learners to determine the content and the method
- to be the principal resource for the learners' learning
- to be solely responsible for the learning that takes place
- to ensure that the group works as a group
- to allow learners to explore and digress
- to be seen as a manager of learning opportunities.

Activity 5.7

Your way is OK

This activity is especially useful at the start of a course or session. Initially, learners will be wondering how they will be expected to behave and to respond to the course. For instance, some may be worried that they will not understand the content, while others may be concerned that they will have to agree, or comply, with the content and everything the teacher says. You can help to remove the potential block this state can cause by making a statement which recognizes that they will feel or think or behave in a range of ways and that these are normal and acceptable. You are in effect saying that it is OK for all to react in their own way.

Think of a session you ran recently. What could you have said to let your learners know that their way of **behaving** was OK?

Example:

'You may be uncertain whether you need to take notes. Everything I show you on a slide I will be giving you on a handout, so you do not have to take notes but, of course, you may choose to anyway.'

Your example:

Think of a session you ran recently. What could you have said to let your learners know that their way of **thinking** was OK?

Example:

'When I have run this session before, some learners have found the topic quite useful to know about, others have found that the model doesn't work for them, and a few have said that it totally transformed their approach to the subject. It will be interesting to see whether you fall into one of those categories.'

Your example:

Think of a session you ran recently. What could you have said to let your learners know that their way of **feeling** was OK?

Example:

'Don't worry if you are shocked by the ideas I will give you today; I remember that I was when I first heard them on a course, because they didn't seem to make sense.'

Your example:

Chapter 6

Acknowledging individual learners

This chapter includes the following activities:

6.1 How far do I currently acknowledge individual learners?
6.2 Using learners' names

What does it mean and why does it matter?

One simple but very important way in which you can affect a learner's feelings for the better is to acknowledge the learner's existence. We all need to be acknowledged and we normally are, in our family, social and work groupings. Even if sometimes we do not like how we are perceived by others, at least we know that they are aware of us. However, in a group of learners there is a strong possibility that we will not be acknowledged, and this can leave us with an unsatisfactory sense of not belonging.

The concept of 'strokes' from Transactional Analysis (TA) is helpful here. (There is more on strokes in Chapter 10.) TA tells us that a stroke is a 'unit of recognition' (Stewart and Joines 1987: 72). It is when one person acknowledges the existence of another, verbally or non-verbally, positively or negatively. You 'give someone a stroke' when you say 'Hello' or smile at them or even frown at them. It is based on Eric Berne's concept of *recognition hunger* (ibid.). He suggests that when we are babies we thrive on physical attention and normally receive a sufficiency of it, through being picked up, played with and cuddled. Ian Stewart and Vann Joines (ibid.) cite studies of babies in a children's home, which indicate that the lack of this physical attention has an adverse effect on us both emotionally and physically. As we grow older, we still have this need, but we often substitute forms of recognition other than the physical. We all need strokes and *any stroke, even a negative one, is better than no stroke at all*. Simply being acknowledged can affect your emotional state for the better.

A study at Staffordshire University (Thomas 2002) found that students in higher education in the UK were more likely to drop out of their studies because of lack of a sense of belonging rather than, as is commonly supposed, because of lack of finance. This belonging depended on relationships with other students but also relationships with lecturers. 'If you go to a lecture and you answer one of their questions, and they say, "What's your name?" it just doesn't feel like they value your presence. If they can't be bothered to learn my name . . .' (ibid.: 433). The Staffordshire study indicates that we should do more in the classroom to help individuals feel they belong. I suspect this need not even go as far as valuing individuals; acknowledgement alone, in a positive or negative way, will make the learner more likely to stay.

Staff in further and higher education who are concerned about retention make plans, quite justifiably, about selection procedures, course design, assessment, feedback strategies and student support and guidance in order to improve the retention rate. The aspect of the learners' experience that it is quite easy to overlook, however, is the immediate impact of what happens in the classroom. When this part of the learners' experience leaves them feeling that they are fully acknowledged, and hopefully valued and respected too, they are more likely to maintain motivation and engagement in their learning experience.

In the classroom there are three levels at which you can acknowledge learners:

- eye contact;
- using learners' names;
- referring to previous contributions.

Eye contact

Ask yourself, do you make a point of making eye contact with every person in your class? Or do you, like so many of us, unwittingly concentrate on those more receptive, welcoming faces? I have witnessed teachers who connect with one face in the room and stay fixed on it for far too long. The effect would be almost comical if it were not potentially so upsetting for most of the learners. The recipient of the teacher's look becomes more anxious and more ready to please, feeling they have to respond to the teacher's talk on behalf of the whole group. The rest of the group start to question whether they are truly there, as the teacher has taken no notice of them for so long. On other occasions it is just the few who are immediately to the teacher's left or right who are excluded from eye contact and who start to feel invisible. For the teacher, it requires a conscious effort to look at everyone, even if some do not return your gaze.

Using learners' names

The use or non-use of learners' names always has an impact on how they feel about their learning and on the climate in the room. Learners who are never addressed by name by the teacher are likely to feel very differently from those who are. Most learners value this recognition greatly. It shows that you have identified their presence as an individual. Even mature, confident learners will welcome this.

I acknowledge that in some circumstances, especially if you are a university lecturer, you have too many students in a session and/or too many different groups in a week for you ever to be able to know or use all names. But if your group sizes are 30 or less, it should be possible to know and use everyone's name. Teachers often say, 'I'm no good with names' but I am convinced that it depends on how motivated you are to learn them. Instead of saying, 'I wish I could remember names' or 'It would be nice to use them', you need to say, 'It is essential that I use names' and act accordingly. That means putting more energy into remembering and using names. It means deliberately planning the beginning of a session with a new group so that you have the opportunity to learn and use names. If you perceive that using names is the most important thing you do in the first hour with a new group, that in itself will make it more likely to happen. Activity 6.2 below suggests one way of doing this. If you do have far too many in your group to remember their names, it may be worth explaining this to the group. You might then choose to ask the names of individuals when they speak and use their names at the same time.

You may sometimes work in a situation that uses 'delegate cards', with each learner's name written on a card in front of them. Of course these are useful for group members. Be wary of relying on them yourself, however. This can make you lazy about learning names and you find yourself taking time to read the card before you speak to the learner.

I was impressed whilst observing a lecturer with a group of around 70 that he was able to use the names of learners who asked questions. He explained to me that he had been able to obtain the photos of group members from the student record office and he was able to learn them gradually before and after sessions. If you are going to be seeing a group on a number of occasions, consider taking everyone's photograph, with their permission of course, during the first session. You can then keep a copy of their photographs with names. You may even be able to distribute, or put on a website, copies of the photographs for everyone in the group, again subject to their permission.

An incidental benefit of getting to know names is that it forces you to acknowledge to yourself that this is a collection of individuals and not 'year 3' or whatever category you have assigned to them all. It also assists you greatly in controlling classroom activity. For example, you can say, 'Let's hear from Jo, then Kiran and then Richard.' If you want to exercise some control over the composition of small groups, it is invaluable to be able to direct this by using names.

Referring to previous contributions

Knowing names also helps in the final level of acknowledging learners – referring to what individuals have said before. Make a conscious effort to refer to the contributions of individuals in the group, such as, 'As Alex pointed out earlier'; or 'This next section deals with Chris's important question of a few minutes ago.' You don't need to do this, but the positive impact on the individuals concerned can be very potent.

Acknowledging individuals is one of those behaviours that you may well be doing spontaneously. I suggest, however, that it is important to become conscious of what you do about this and to monitor your behaviour. You should treat it as a vital part of the use of emotional intelligence with learners, and you should do it consciously and deliberately.

There are two activities in the remainder of this chapter. Activity 6.1 invites you to review your current practice in acknowledging individual learners, while Activity 6.2 suggests a technique for remembering names.

Investigating your practice

Activity 6.1

How far do I currently acknowledge individual learners?

To review your current practice in acknowledging individuals, think of the last group you taught. Ask yourself the following questions:

1   Did I make eye contact with all members of the group?
2   Did I find myself making eye contact with some members of the group more than others? If so, why was that?
3   Do I know everyone's name?
4   How have I come to know the names I do?
5   Did I use everyone's name?
6   How often did I refer to individual contributions?

Developing your practice

Activity 6.2

Using learners' names

This activity suggests a series of steps intended to help you to remember and use the names of a new group of up to 30 learners.

1.   If you are able, speak with as many individuals as you can and find out their names before the session starts. For example, you could make time to greet them.
2.   Ensure that each person is introduced to the whole group in the first 20 minutes of the session. This may be done just as some form of introduction or as a follow-up to an icebreaker where each introduces their partner. This is the point at which you should write down learners' names.

3. While you are listening to these introductions, you may also be able to recite mentally the names you have already heard.

4. At the end of each introduction, take the opportunity to use that person's name, for example, 'Thank you, Sarah.'

5. Ensure that learners engage in another activity within the following 30 minutes and arrange that, while they are busy, you will have the time then to go through their names. Do it like this: look at each person and see whether you remember their name. Say the name to yourself while looking at the person. If you have to read it from your list, say it to yourself again while looking at them.

6. Eventually go around the whole group saying their names to yourself.

7. When their activity has finished, make sure that you use at least some of the names, if not all.

8. Later, check which names you have not used and make sure you use them before the session is over.

This method assists you in memorizing because you are learning by hearing, writing, speaking and reading the names.

Many teachers say that they are far too preoccupied with what they have to say or what they need to get learners to do and that there is no time to concentrate on names. It is a question of priorities, and if you rate the use of names as important, you must devote time and energy to planning for using and remembering them.

Chapter 7

Listening to your learners

This chapter includes the following activities:

7.1 Using listening skills with groups of learners
7.2 Listening badly
7.3 Whose frame of reference?
7.4 Analysing a listener's responses

What does it mean and why does it matter?

In preparing to be a teacher, a great deal of your energy goes into learning how to talk to groups. In your role, you will need to explain, direct and inform, and many courses on becoming an effective teacher include components on presentation skills, how to project your voice and so on. The complementary skill of listening is just as important as talking but is often overlooked. Teachers need to know how to listen. The ability to listen, to attend to others, is an integral component of emotional intelligence.

There are some excellent courses on listening skills. They usually assume that you are going to use the skills in listening to one person at a time, as in counselling. However, it is possible, and I would say essential, to adapt these listening skills and include them as part of your practice with whole groups of learners or with individuals who are part of a group.

There are very specific skills that you can use as a listener, known as active listening skills. These include: paraphrasing, reflecting feelings, using open questions, demonstrating empathy and managing silence. There are more details on these in Activity 7.1 later in this chapter. Effective use of these skills requires that you are fully attentive to the speaker and are not impeded by your own concerns or impatience. You need to hear what they are saying and you also need to hear what they are communicating to you but not necessarily articulating.

Using these skills with groups can have the same effects as when using them with individuals:

- Learners derive great benefit simply from being heard properly.
- You have a better understanding of the learners' perspective and can tailor your material accordingly.
- You can use listening skills to foster genuinely learner-centred approaches, where your role is to help learners find answers and solutions independently.
- Listening helps in building a good relationship. A good relationship depends on dialogue, and dialogue in turn depends upon the ability to truly listen to and understand the perspective of the other person.

The emotionally intelligent teacher will go into a session just as ready to listen as to talk. What you say in a session should be determined as much by what the learners say in the session as by what you have planned to say. It is usually expected by you and by the learners that if they make a comment or ask a question, you will respond with your expertise. But sometimes your readiness to jump in with your own analysis or wealth of anecdotes and experiences can take away from what the learner is actually saying. You can fail to truly value the learners' experience and sometimes not even hear correctly what they have said because of your rush to contribute. Of course, listening skills do not readily translate into all learning contexts; for example, there are limited opportunities to use them when lecturing to a large group. However, if you are genuinely seeking to facilitate learning, you need to be practised at knowing when to listen and when to talk.

Good listening is both disciplined and spontaneous. Obviously no response can be planned in advance (although you may anticipate frequently-asked questions). When you have heard a learner's comment or question you need to choose your response very carefully, selecting from your repertoire of skills, looking for the one that will best serve you in assisting them to reach their goals. Being a good listener is a prerequisite to showing you are responding to people's feelings (see Chapter 8) and to handling responses (see Chapter 9).

Most of what is taught on listening skills today has its roots in the work of Carl Rogers. On the basis of his work as a clinical psychologist in the 1920s, Rogers formulated his theory known as 'client-centred therapy'. He held that, if a psychotherapist wanted to assist their client in changing, the relationship that existed between the therapist and client was more important than the therapist's expertise in the type of problem. If the therapist could exhibit the qualities of *genuineness*, *empathy* and *acceptance*, and if the client could acknowledge those qualities, then change would occur in the client (Rogers 1961: 33–4). The role of the therapist was to assist the client in finding their own solution to whatever problem had brought them to therapy by exhibiting the three qualities mentioned above and, in so doing, fully listening to the client. The listening approach in person-centred counselling derives from the work of Carl Rogers and is to be found in many listening skills courses, even if Rogers's influence is not always acknowledged.

Rogers soon suggested that what was true in the therapy room could apply in the classroom too: 'If the creation of an atmosphere of acceptance, understanding and respect is the most effective basis for facilitating the learning which is called therapy, then might it not be the basis for the learning which is called education?' (Rogers 1951: 384).

The research conducted to test his principles in education has included work by David Aspy and Flora Roebuck. They investigated the impact on student effectiveness of the teacher who exhibited genuineness, empathy and acceptance. After assessing 3700 hours of classroom instruction by 550 elementary and secondary schoolteachers, they concluded: '*Students learn more and behave better when they receive high levels of understanding, caring and genuineness, than when they are given low levels of them.* It pays to treat students as sensitive and aware human beings' (Aspy and Roebuck 1983: 199; emphasis in original).

Rogers himself was wary of teaching the skills without considering the person who was using them. He saw that procedures and techniques are less important than attitudes, as noted above (page 10). Like all aspects of emotional intelligence, developing as an effective listener requires time to practise and the opportunity for structured reflection on your experience.

This chapter continues with activities that give you the opportunity to begin to explore your use of listening skills as a teacher. If you want to pursue the development of your listening skills, consider taking a course, rather than further reading, because of the opportunities for practice and feedback.

Investigating your practice

Activity 7.1

Using listening skills with groups of learners

This activity helps you identify the extent to which you currently use listening skills, which are normally used with one person, with groups or with individuals in groups.

Here is a list of skills and qualities used in active listening. Complete the questionnaire to establish which of these skills you use when working with a group.

A = I never do this   B = I do this occasionally   C = I do this frequently

	A	B	C
Asking open questions	☐	☐	☐

This means asking questions which invite an answer other than 'yes' or 'no'.
Example: 'What do you think of the idea I have
        just outlined?'

	A	B	C
Paraphrasing	☐	☐	☐

This means repeating to the speaker what they have just said, possibly changing the words but retaining the meaning.
Example: A learner says, 'I realize now the relevance
        of this part of the session.'
You reply by paraphrasing, 'so the relevance of this part is now clear'.

	A	B	C
Reflecting feelings	☐	☐	☐

This means to reflect back to the speaker the feelings they are conveying to you.
Example: 'You sound as though you are both surprised
        and relieved to hear this.'

	A	B	C
Demonstrating empathy	☐	☐	☐

This means to show the speaker that you have an appreciation of their perspective.
Example: 'You must be very anxious about being
        here today.'

	A	B	C
Managing silence	☐	☐	☐

This means to maintain attention but not speak immediately after someone stops speaking.
Example: A learner says 'I think some of our managers
        would benefit from coming on this course.'
        The teacher does not speak but maintains eye
        contact with the learner and perhaps nods or
        raises an eyebrow. This gives the learner the
        chance to elaborate or for someone else in
        the group to respond. The teacher could
        continue to communicate just non-verbally
        through facial expression, posture and in this
        way invite comments from others.

	A	B	C
Clarifying	☐	☐	☐

This means to check that you have heard accurately what the speaker has said.
Example: 'Let me make sure I understand what you
        are saying – your main concern is ...'

Activity 7.2

Listening badly

Everyday conventions in listening differ from the more disciplined approach that characterizes active listening. This activity helps you to recognize some types of everyday listening that are not good practice in active listening.

Here are seven different ways in which individuals can demonstrate that they are not truly listening.

Behaviour	Typical phrase
Denying the speaker's feelings	'Cheer up, it could be worse'
Shifting the focus to themselves	'That happened to me once and ..'
Asking too many questions and interrupting too often to enable the speaker to express themselves fully	'When did this happen?' 'How come?' 'Did you say this was last week? What day?'
Jumping to a solution	'What you need to do is …'
Taking over responsibility rather than hearing any more	'Don't worry, I'll sort it out.'
Simply failing to show interest	'Oh, really?' (whilst continuing to look at their computer screen)
Denying the power of the speaker's feeling	'You shouldn't get so worked up about it.'

It is likely that in your day-to-day exchanges you have failed to listen in some or all of these ways at some time. You may even have done it deliberately as a strategy to shut the other person up.

1.   Identify those you use most frequently yourself.

2.   Which of these styles have you used when listening to a learner?

3.   Are there any you could justify using when listening to a learner?

Developing your practice

Activity 7.3

Whose frame of reference?

A prerequisite for responding to feelings expressed by others is the ability to step outside of our 'frame of reference' and into that of the other person. If we can also communicate to the other person that we are doing this, we are likely to make it easier for them to explain or express more and for dialogue and understanding to develop.

Each of the four statements below is given three possible responses. For each response, identify whether it takes the frame of reference of the person who made the statement (the 'speaker') or the frame of reference of the person who responds (the 'listener'). For response 'D', insert the kind of response *you* would typically make.

1.   **Learner to teacher**
     I'm thinking of giving up the course. I find it very hard to fit everything in.

A   So you're thinking of leaving the course because of the difficulties you have in getting everything done.
B   You're not giving it a chance.
C   So you're pushed for time – you should have seen this coming.
D

2.   **Teacher to teacher**
     That group I've just had are a difficult bunch this year. I can't get them to join in at all.

A   Well, it's still early days, they'll come round, I'm sure.
B   You're saying you can't get them to participate.
C   *I'm* getting on fine with them.
D

3. **Teacher to teacher**
   I spend more time on admin and form-filling than I do on teaching. It's not what I came into this for.

A   You're saying that you are not spending enough time on what's important for you.
B   I can see you're not happy with how things are, but never mind, it's not so long now until you can retire.
C   There's work to be done and we've got to make the most of it. Times change.
D

4. **Learner to teacher**
   I found this course difficult at first but now it is very worthwhile.

A   I'm very pleased myself with the group and how they are working.
B   So you're getting a lot out of it.
C   I wish there were more like you.
D

Comments

1A This reflects the speaker's frame of reference and paraphrases what was said.
1B This is the listener's frame of reference; it rushes to a judgement and tells the speaker that the listener is not ready to listen.
1C This starts with the learner's frame of reference but moves to an assumption which may or may not be justified but almost certainly doesn't help the learner.
2A A kindly but dismissive response, more about the listener's need to make the speaker either feel better or just shut up.
2B This takes the speaker's frame of reference and makes it easier for them to say more.
2C The listener's frame of reference and no help at all.
3A An accurate paraphrase of what was said, from the speaker's frame of reference.
3B Starts with the speaker's frame of reference but moves on to satisfying the listener's need to reassure them.
3C The listener's frame of reference.
4A Doesn't negate what they said but comes from the listener's frame of reference.
4B Speaker's frame of reference.
4C Again, this does not override what they said but is about the listener not the speaker.

Of course it would be inappropriate, not to say bizarre, to be perpetually responding from the frame of reference of others, particularly if all you are doing is repeating back to them what they have already said. What is important is to ensure that you have the ability to do this, i.e. to listen *fully* and to empathize, which enlarges your repertoire of responses and leads to more effective communication.

Activity 7.4

Analysing a listener's responses

This activity builds on the three activities above to look at listening in action. It gives you the opportunity to suggest how to improve this teacher's use of listening skills.

At the end of a session, a learner comes up to the teacher. The learner is a student who is experiencing personal problems at home. Their exchange goes like this:

1. *Learner:* Can I speak to you about my coursework?
2. *Teacher:* I don't really have time now – I need to get ready for my next session.
3. *L:* It's just that I'm struggling to finish it by the deadline ...
4. *T:* I have an office hour tomorrow morning. You could come and see me then.
5. *L:* OK.
6. *T:* But if it's just an extension you want, I could give you an extra two days. Could you get it finished by then?
7. *L:* Well, it's just that I'm trying to juggle so many things at the moment. My mum is in hospital and I need to visit her every day as well as looking after my little brother.
8. *T:* I'm sorry to hear that. But the extra time will help you. Is that OK?
9. *L:* I suppose.
10. *T:* You know I can't give extensions for any longer than that.
11. *L:* Yes, it's just that I haven't had time to go to the library yet, let alone start to write it.
12. *T:* Have you been to see the support officer? They'll be able to help you apply for a longer extension.
13. *L:* I thought about it but I don't know where their office is.
14. *T:* You can look it up on the internet. In the meantime at least you can work on your essay knowing you've got the extension you wanted.
15. *L:* I suppose. I'll try and find the time to go.
16. *T:* And remember to pay close attention to the question when you're working on your answer. A lot of people don't!
17. *L :* OK ...
18. *T:* And don't forget my office hour as well if you need more help. Right, I need to get to my next seminar.

1. Look critically at the teacher's responses. Make a note of the lines where you think the teacher should have done or said something different.
2. For each line that you have chosen, write *why* you think the teacher should have done or said something different.
3. For each line you have chosen, suggest exactly what the teacher should have done or said differently – what you feel would have been a better (more emotionally intelligent) response.

Chapter 8

Reading and responding to the feelings of individuals and groups

This chapter includes the following activities:

8.1 Reviewing your current practice
8.2 Demonstrating group empathy
8.3 How is it for you?
8.4 Reading learners' non-verbal communication and reflecting feelings
8.5 Responding to feelings as well as to the problem presented

What does it mean and why does it matter?

This book is based on the premise that emotions are bound up with learning, and so being able to read and respond to your learners' feelings is a core component of using emotional intelligence in teaching. There will be times when learners convey feelings to you, intentionally or otherwise. To use emotional intelligence in your teaching includes showing that you can read, acknowledge and respond to these feelings, especially the negative ones.

Indeed, if you have taken the steps suggested in earlier chapters to provide the right environment, learners will be more likely to express their feelings.

Be ready to attend to this and to have dialogue with your learners that is about their feelings, to the extent that those feelings are bound up with their learning. This includes attempting to take account of how they feel even if they are not necessarily expressing this strongly. Activity 8.2 below, 'demonstrating group empathy', is an example of this.

So much of teaching is based on the assumption that the learners are present cognitively but not otherwise. If you want to be more effective in your role, such an assumption will be constraining. The whole person is engaged in learning and you should be addressing, and be ready to relate to, the whole of the learner. To ignore their feelings is to ignore a significant part of them as a learner. So the focus of this chapter is an extension of the listening skills discussed in the previous chapter.

To listen fully to someone includes listening to facts and feelings alike. Those feelings may be articulated by the person you are listening to or may be implicit in what they are communicating to you, unsaid yet still conveyed. It was Albert Mehrabian's work that confirmed the significance of factors other than the words spoken when someone attempts to convey feelings and attitudes. He gave figures to indicate the relative importance of each of three factors – 7 per cent to the words spoken; 38 per cent to the way the words are said; and 55 per cent to the facial expression of the speaker. These were very specifically for application when the speaker was talking about their feelings and attitudes and are not necessarily transferable to other examples of communication. Clearly they are of most use when there is incongruence between factors and so the advice from his findings is, to pay more attention to the facial expression than to the tone of voice and more to the tone of voice than to the words. More detail can be found on Mehrabian's website, www.kaaj.com/psych/.

What you can achieve through reading and responding to feelings is to let your learners know that:

- you recognize that they have feelings;
- it is okay to express those feelings;
- you are ready to accept those feelings;
- you can respond on this level as well as on a cognitive level.

Many of the occasions when teachers claim they have 'difficult' learners stem from the teacher's inability or reluctance to acknowledge the learner's feelings. If a learner is experiencing negative feelings and these are not attended to, that learner will be using up energy that could instead be used for learning. There is then a likelihood that their original show of negative feeling will be compounded by mistrust or resentment towards you because of the way you failed to acknowledge and handle it. So, acknowledging or failing to acknowledge feelings will have a significant effect on a learner's responsiveness and readiness to learn. Obviously, it will also affect the emotional environment in the classroom. How you fail to deal with one learner's feelings will send a message to other members of the group and, in turn, affect their behaviour.

You may think that the classroom is not the place to start talking about feelings. I certainly would not suggest that you become a counsellor, ready to deal with the range of feelings an individual has and to assist them with their personal problems. That is not your job, and it would be inappropriate and damaging behaviour, so be sure to have a clear understanding of your limits in this respect. To teach with emotional intelligence includes being ready to acknowledge and respond to the feelings of learners and also knowing how far it is appropriate to do so. By dealing with your learners' feelings:

- the learners will feel valued;
- it helps you to develop a fuller relationship with them;
- it aids their learning;
- it helps to shape a positive environment.

Activity 8.1 asks you to begin to think about your current practice in reading and dealing with learners' feelings. Activities 8.2, 8.3 and 8.4 suggest strategies you can try with learners, while 8.5 is an exercise in picking up on a learner's feelings conveyed in writing.

Investigating your practice

Activity 8.1

Reviewing your current practice

This is a brief activity that invites you to begin to review what you currently do to read and respond to the feelings of learners.

Think back to the most recent session you have run. Ask these questions:

1. Was I aware of the overall mood of the group at any point during the session?
2. How did I sense that mood?
3. Did I respond to that mood?
4. Was I aware at any time of the feelings of any individual learner?
5. How did I become aware of those feelings?
6. How did I respond to those feelings?
7. Is there anything more I could have done to be aware of, and then respond to, the mood of the group and the feelings of individual learners?

Developing your practice

Activity 8.2

Demonstrating group empathy

Empathy means the ability to see the world as it looks to someone else. However, it is important to remember that while you can have some sense of how another person is feeling and experiencing, you can never see things in exactly the same way as them. Furthermore, simply being empathic will have no impact on the other person unless you demonstrate your empathy by conveying to them that you have an understanding of how they feel. Demonstrating your empathy with another can help them feel better, just to know that someone is in tune with them and understands. It also gives them the opportunity to 'correct' your perception of their feelings if you are 'wrong'.

You can demonstrate empathy with a group of learners. This means it is possible to say something to the group that shows that you have a sense of how at least some of them are feeling at a given point. You can show that you both acknowledge and accept their feelings. Demonstrating to learners that you are ready and able to see things from their perspective can greatly increase their responsiveness and readiness to engage with the session.

Here are some examples of group empathy statements:

> 'At this stage of the course I suspect most of you will be concerned about the exam.'

> 'From your response to the activity that we did last week, I sense you will be relieved to know that this week there is no role-playing, just discussion groups.'

> 'My guess is that a number of you will be anxious to start work on how to apply the mass of information you've received so far.'

If you use a statement that acknowledges a negative feeling, remember to be ready to follow it up with a positive statement. Here is an example.

The teacher says to the learners at the beginning of a one-day professional development course:

> 'I know some of you have not chosen to be here today and so I imagine some of you are thinking, "I would rather be getting on with my backlog of work than sitting here for a day." '

The teacher continues:

> 'So I am keen to ensure we make the best use of your valuable time and that you gain something useful from today – and I will be checking with you as we go along to make sure it's relevant and that you can make use of it.'

Think of a session you have run recently. Write five examples of group empathy statements that you could have used or did use and, where appropriate, a follow-up positive statement.

Activity 8.3

How is it for you?

This is an activity that can give reassurance and clarification to learners, as well as providing feedback for you on how things are going. It is another technique for developing dialogue between you and your learners.

When teaching, you may experience sessions in which you cannot tell how the material is being received by learners. By asking them how they feel and responding appropriately, you can:

• provide a welcome break in the session;

- show that you value how they feel and that you can accept their feelings;
- receive feedback which might result in you revisiting part of the course or even modifying what you have planned for the remainder of the session.

1. Say to your learners:
   'As I look at your faces, it's difficult for me to tell what your response is so far.'
2. Then say:
   'Take a few seconds to think of the one word which best describes how you feel about what we have covered so far. For example, the word might be "fascinated", "confused", "bored", "intrigued" – just use whatever word sums it up best for you. It is okay to say "pass".'
3. Hear each person's word in turn. Don't encourage them to say more than one word. Don't comment on any of their responses, except to acknowledge them and perhaps say, 'Thank you'.
4. When you have all their words, consider your response. Here are some examples of what they might say and how you might respond:

If they used words such as:

'fascinated', 'intrigued', 'excited', 'stimulated', 'exhilarated'

you could say:

'Good. In that case I'm sure you'll really appreciate what comes next.'

If they used words such as:

'confused', 'puzzled', 'uncertain', 'overwhelmed'

you could say:

'Could you tell me more about what you have found puzzling?'

If they used words such as:

'bored', 'detached', 'not bothered', 'it's okay', 'nothing'

you could say:

'What would you say would make it more interesting for you?'

If they used words such as:

'interested', 'curious', 'open-minded', 'motivated'

you could say:

'That's great. I think you will find this next activity very rewarding.'

If they used words such as:

'frustrated', 'impatient', 'uncomfortable'

you could say:

'Could you say what the source of your frustration is?'

Activity 8.4

Reading learners' non-verbal communication and reflecting feelings

You can gain a useful sense of the mood of a group of learners by reading their non-verbal communication. This information gives you another chance to connect with the group because, on the basis of your reading of their non-verbal communication, you can reflect their feelings. Statements that reflect feelings usually start with phrases like, 'I sense that . . .', 'it seems to me that you feel . . .'. This activity gives a checklist of non-verbal communication to look out for and asks you to practise how you would reflect the feelings you see.

1. Take stock of the mood of the group by asking yourself these five questions. Place a tick by the most suitable word(s). You may want to add words of your own.

---

a) What is the posture of your learners, whether seated or standing?

upright   ☐
slouching   ☐
open   ☐
defensive   ☐

b) What is the direction of their gaze, both when you are talking and when they are doing activities?

towards you   ☐
towards others ☐
looking down   ☐
looking away   ☐

c)   What is the typical facial expression of group members?

engaged   ☐
frowning   ☐
smiling   ☐
blank   ☐

d)   What is the dominant tone of voice from the group during activities and question and answer?

lively   ☐
tired   ☐
resigned   ☐
enquiring   ☐

e)   How do the learners move in forming small groups and in carrying out activities?

briskly   ☐
slowly   ☐
reluctantly   ☐
enthusiastically   ☐

2.   Now reflect the feelings of your learners:

Here are some suggested responses that attempt to reflect their feelings.

If you have ticked:	*upright; towards you; smiling; lively; briskly*
you could say:	*'There's a real buzz in the room today. People seem to be finding this very useful. Am I right?'*
If you have ticked:	*slouching; looking down; blank; tired; slowly*
you could say:	*'I guess you are not getting as much from this as usual. It looks like I need to bring forward an activity I had planned for later.'*
If you have ticked:	*defensive; looking away; frowning; resigned; reluctantly*
you could say:	*'I sense that some of you are not happy with the session so far. Anyone care to comment?'*
If you have ticked:	*open; towards others; engaged; enquiring; enthusiastic*
you could say:	*'I can see there is a great deal of interest in this topic.'*
If you have ticked:	*upright; towards you; frowning; resigned; slowly*
you could say:	*'I am getting mixed messages from you about today's session.'*

Remember always to be cautious in interpreting body language. For instance, a learner who is always looking out of the window while you are talking to the class could indicate to you a lack of attention. Yet, for some learners, looking away can be a useful strategy for concentrating. Also, take care if your group includes learners from different cultures. Two learners may exhibit the same gesture or expression but the intended meaning may be different.

Activity 8.5

Responding to feelings as well as to the problem presented

This activity asks you to put yourself in the position of a teacher who has received an email from a student. The student, Ellen, is in work and is studying part-time on a master's degree programme and you are her dissertation supervisor. Having read the email, you will prepare for a tutorial with her next week. When you meet, there will be obvious points of information and guidance to offer Ellen, but first it is important to recognize what feelings Ellen is expressing in her message and to acknowledge them. This is necessary as they may well be what is most important for her, and if you ignore them it will affect the quality of communication in your tutorial with Ellen. She will be more likely to hear and more ready to learn if you have clearly responded to the emotional content of her email first.

Here is the email:

> I am getting in touch as promised, in advance of our tutorial scheduled for next week, to bring you up to date. I've had the questionnaires back now and I was pleased at the number who returned them. But at first glance they don't seem to be saying what I hoped they would, which is a worry. Actually I'm at a loss as to how to collate the data, both qualitative and quantitative. I know we talked about it, and it seemed clear then, but I'd like some guidance. I've drafted how I think I should approach the interviews. Mind you, it might be irrelevant because my boss is going back on what she said. We agreed I could have a day a fortnight to do this, especially the interviews, but now she says that won't be possible, at least not before Christmas. She's so unreliable!! I don't see now how I can do the follow-up interviews, and that puts my schedule right behind. I just can't see how it's going to happen. What with some things going on at home too it's all a bit overwhelming. Anyway, see you Monday, Ellen.

Remember, you are confident about the technical advice you need to give Ellen on her dissertation, but in preparing for your meeting with her, ask yourself:

1. What feelings are conveyed by Ellen in her email?
2. How will you acknowledge and deal with these feelings when you meet, before going further and discussing her problems with her studies?

Chapter 9

Responding to learners' comments and questions

This chapter includes the following activities:

9.1 Acceptant responses
9.2 Prefacing your response
9.3 Taking control of transactions
9.4 Responding to provocative comments
9.5 Your use of language in responses
9.6 Paying attention to the tone of your written responses

What does it mean and why does it matter?

Each occasion on which a learner makes a comment or asks a question provides an opportunity for you to use emotional intelligence in the way you respond. Depending on the circumstances, you may have the chance to:

- affect how they feel about being in that session;
- determine whether they will speak again in the session;
- influence how they feel about themselves as learners;
- influence how they view you;
- influence how the rest of the group view you and the session;
- confirm the kind of relationship you have with your learners.

If handled well, your response can:

- improve the motivation of the individual and other learners;
- affect the emotional environment for the better;
- clarify what kinds of question or comment from learners are acceptable;
- show the learners that you value their responses;
- show the learners that you are listening.

Obviously you cannot plan for dealing with responses; if you had to stop to deliberate each response you make in terms of all of the above factors, you would be incapable of responding normally. However, the significance of these exchanges between you and your learners, beyond the simple exchange of information, is very easy to underestimate. How you respond could be the most obvious indicator to your learners of how you view them.

In formulating your response, it is useful to think on two levels – the affective and the cognitive. The cognitive is one on which we are accustomed to responding as teachers. You can decide to inform, clarify, agree, expand or correct; in other words, give a response to do with the intellect. You can seek to develop the learner's train of thought by asking a question in response, inviting others to respond, making a link with what has been said before and so on.

The affective level means asking yourself whether you wish to have an effect on the feelings of the questioner (and others). Should you attempt to make them feel respected, valued, enthused, belittled, dismissed or humiliated? It is likely you will have an effect regardless – it is rarely possible to avoid having any affective impact. If you concentrate on your cognitive response without taking into account your affective impact, there is the possibility of causing problems. Your cognitive response may be accurate while your affective response may be damaging or clumsy.

One common way to seek a positive affective impact is to praise. However, praise should be used with caution; a better goal in terms of emotional intelligence is to be non-judgemental, which means neither to condemn nor to praise. The point about being non-judgemental is that when you respond to a learner, you do not encourage them to depend on *your* judgement of their contribution and their success. Part of your role is to assist them in making *their own* judgements about their learning. Eric Jensen cites research by both Alfie Kohn and Roy Baumeister about the possible negative effects of too much praise. He concludes, 'The most striking and permanent interpretation of a positive judgement is that it is still a judgement' (Jensen 1995: 268). Creating too much learner dependency on your judgements makes for an emotionally unhealthy relationship between you and the learners. Feedback and encouragement, from you or from the learners' peers, are more useful.

Hopefully, every question or comment from a learner is made in good faith and you can take it at face value. However, there is every chance that learners, through what they say and how they say it, will invite you to respond in a particular way that suits their purposes. Michael Maynard identifies a range of examples of difficult learners (Maynard 2003): the Attacker, the Sniper, the Rebel, the Incredible Sulk and so on. They may or may not be aware of what they are doing, but you have to be. You also have to gauge your response carefully with an eye to its effect on them, on the rest of the group, on you and on the purpose of the session. For example, the learner says, 'Have we *really* got to complete this task?' ('really' said in a pleading tone). This is more than a straightforward question. It is inviting you to make an indulgent response such as, 'Well, not if you don't want to' or 'Well, do what you can, it doesn't matter if you don't do it all.' There are two concepts, which have their origin in Transactional Analysis (known as TA, see Chapter 2), that are very useful for understanding what is going on in this example and for guiding us in how to respond. They are called 'personal styles' (or 'ego-states') and 'transactions'. Essentially the learner is (probably unconsciously) trying to provoke you into behaving in a certain way that they will feel more comfortable with. They are trying to call the shots in the relationship you have with them. You need to be aware of this possibility and to give the response you want to and take control of the transactions (see Activity 9.3).

The same principles about responding to learners apply if you have to give feedback on an assessment, whether it is a presentation or a written assignment. Of course, you are obliged to give the cognitive response, probably including diagnosis, guidance and advice. But you can provide the same cognitive response while varying your affective response greatly. In other words, it's not just what you say, but how you say it. And how you say it will determine whether the recipient, your learner, truly hears what you say. Activity 9.6 gives the opportunity to reshape the affective message in some written feedback.

Almost all of the remainder of this chapter offers suggestions on how to make the most of your responses to learners. Before that, in *Investigating your practice*, there are a few questions on how you currently handle learners' questions and comments.

Investigating your practice

The following are useful questions to ask in appraising your current practice in responding to learners.

1. How far do I take note of the likely affective impact of my responses to learners' questions and comments?
2. Do I use my responses to achieve anything more than providing information or developing learners' understanding?
3. Am I aware of any learner comments or questions which intend an additional meaning, perhaps inviting me to respond in a particular way?

Developing your practice

Activity 9.1

Acceptant responses

When a learner asks a question or makes a comment, you may or may not agree with what they say, but it is important to make an acceptant response, i.e. a response which, at the very least, acknowledges and doesn't deny the point of view or feeling that the learner has expressed.

You can do one or both of two things to make an acceptant response.

1. You can acknowledge that that is how the learner thinks or feels:
   'That's perfectly understandable at this point.'
   'That's a very common response from learners when they hear that . . .'
2. You can invite the learner to elaborate and give more information or clarify what they are saying:
   'Tell me more.'
   'What's the nature of your confusion?'

This activity helps you to prepare acceptant responses by first asking you to word the response you should *not* make, i.e. a non-acceptant response.

Here are three examples of comments from learners, each followed by a non-acceptant response, then by an acceptant response.

THE LEARNER SAYS	EXAMPLE OF A NON-ACCEPTANT RESPONSE	EXAMPLE OF AN ACCEPTANT RESPONSE
'I think you are wrong.'	'I think you will find that all of the studies show this to be true.'	'That's interesting. In what way?'
'This course is not providing what I hoped it would.'	'Well, it was quite explicit in the pre-course information that the course was about ...'	'That must be very frustrating. Tell me more about what you were looking for.'
'I'm really excited by the ideas you have given us today.'	'It doesn't always work this well.'	'I'm glad you have found it so rewarding.'

Here are six more learner comments. Take each in turn and create your own example of a non-acceptant response (most people usually find this easier to do!) and then an example of an acceptant response.

THE LEARNER SAYS	YOUR EXAMPLE OF A NON-ACCEPTANT RESPONSE	YOUR EXAMPLE OF AN ACCEPTANT RESPONSE
I'm disappointed that we haven't yet covered ...'		
'The lectures have too much information to take in.'		
'I can't see how this relates to the assessment.'		
'This is the best module I've done for a long time.'		
'I would like less discussion and more information, please.'		
'This is just nothing more than common sense.'		

Activity 9.2

Prefacing your response

This activity looks at how you might make more of any response you give to a learner. Even if your response to a learner's question or comment is straightforward, there is always the opportunity to preface it with a remark intended to make the learner feel good and/or to add to the positive emotional environment. However, be wary of using any such phrase if you do not mean it; avoid the 'have a nice day' syndrome, where there is no congruence between what you say and how you feel.

Here are some examples:

- That's very helpful; it reminds me that . . .
- I'm glad you have said that because . . .
- This is exactly what I was referring to earlier today.
- That leads straight into what we are going to do next.
- You've hit on something very important.
- X has written a whole book about this.
- This is at the heart of what we're talking about.
- It is very useful to ask that question because . . .
- It is essential to ask that question.
- Thanks for drawing our attention to this.

List some more that you would feel able to use.

Activity 9.3

Taking control of transactions

The idea of personal styles and transactions derives from Transactional Analysis (see Activity 2.3). Here's a reminder of example behaviours from each of the five personal styles:

1   Controlling Parent – *directing, firm*
2   Nurturing Parent – *caring, reassuring*
3   Adult – *problem-solving, logical*
4   Natural Child – *spontaneous, creative, fun-loving*
5   Adapted Child – *compliant, polite* or *rebellious, sulking.*

Looking at how personal styles 'transact' with each other provides a framework that we can use to review how we communicate with others. Unconsciously, we may be 'flipped' into a response that is triggered by what others say. More productive exchanges, certainly those more suitable for learning, can come about if we bring these transactions into our consciousness and take some control over them. This activity gives some examples of how you might be provoked into a particular personal style by learners and how you can rehearse responses that do not fuel unproductive transactions. In order to remain in control and to create transactions that help learning, it is useful to be able to determine the most suitable personal style in which to respond.

Example

The learner says:

> 'We don't really need to do every part of this activity, do we?'

This question comes from the rebellious, sulking part of their *Adapted Child*. It might trigger an unconscious response from your *Nurturing Parent* ('No, that's OK') or *Controlling Parent* ('That's not helpful. Please make sure you do all of the task'). In either case, because you have addressed their *Adapted Child*, they will see no reason to change behaviour. They will have been encouraged to look to you to participate in more of the *Adapted Child–Controlling/Nurturing Parent* transactions that they crave, and so will push you into the *Controlling/ Nurturing Parent* role.

Exert more control by ignoring the *Adapted Child* in your learner and addressing their *Adult* from your *Adult*:

> 'Yes. You've got 30 minutes, which is how long it normally takes.'

For each of the following learner statements, phrase a response from the ego-state indicated:

1. Learner: *These activities you get us to do take up far too much time. Don't you think you should take your responsibilities more seriously and just give us the facts?'*
    This comes from *Controlling Parent*, inviting a response from your *Adapted Child*.
    Make a response from your *Adult* to their *Adult*.

2. Learner: *'Don't be concerned about what X (learner) said to you earlier. He's a bit prickly, but we all like you and what you are doing.'*
    This comes from *Nurturing Parent*, inviting a response from your *Natural Child* or *Adapted Child*.
    Make a response from your *Adult* to their *Adult*.

3. Learner: *'Don't you think there's too much jargon and psychobabble in all of this?'*

    This looks like a judgement coming from *Controlling Parent*, probably inviting a response from your *Controlling Parent*.

    Make a response from your *Adult* to their *Adult*.

Your transactions as a teacher do not always have to be *Adult–Adult*. Other transactions can be appropriate. For example, *Controlling Parent–Adapted Child* is suitable when you need to direct your learners. There may be occasions when you join your learners in humour or in creative problem-solving which could be seen as *Natural Child–Natural Child*. The key is that you need to be in control of whichever personal style you inhabit, adept at switching your personal style to suit the purpose, and not be forced into a personal style by learner behaviour.

Activity 9.4

Responding to provocative comments

This activity gives you the chance to explore different responses you could make to a provocative comment from a learner and to work out where each response might lead.

During the session, a learner says to you:

'This is really boring.'

Eight possible responses follow. Take each response in turn and for each one, ask the following questions:

*   What feeling(s) might this provoke in the learner?
*   What might they say next (to you, to another learner and/or to themselves)?
*   Where do you think that will lead?

1. 'That's tough. Let's get on.'
2. Silence: with clenched teeth, big sigh, resigned look.
3. 'Well, leave now then.'
4. 'Well, it's boring for me to hear you say that.'
5. 'Tell me more.'
6. 'I am genuinely glad you feel free to say that. Do you have any suggestions for what would make it more interesting for you?'

7. 'And I guess you're thinking that you have better things to do with your time?'
8. 'I guess you won't be surprised to hear that's a common response when people first encounter this material.'

Activity 9.5

Your use of language in responses

As noted in Chapter 3, the language you use with learners has an effect on their learning state. Even the simplest of questions asked by learners gives you a chance to use positive language in your response and to assist the development of a learning state.

This activity asks you to create responses using positive language. Each example below gives a learner comment or question and a routine response from the teacher. Can you word a teacher response that makes more positive use of language, one which blends the cognitively useful with the affectively positive?

Example

Learner: Are there any books I could read about this?
Teacher response: *The Learning Organization* will do for the basics.
Alternative (more positive) teacher response:
Yes, I recommend *The Learning Organization*, which is an excellent introduction and covers all of the key points. Let me know if you want any more titles.

Produce your own alternative, more positive responses to the examples below, paying particular attention to the language that you use:

Learner: Are there any postgraduate courses in this field?
Teacher response: I have heard the one at X university is OK.
Alternative teacher response:

Learner: Do you think that is a good idea for my dissertation?
Teacher response: I suppose so, but you have to very careful how you introduce it.
Alternative teacher response:

Learner: I am confused by that last point.
Teacher response: That's common. It'll make sense in time.
Alternative teacher response:

Learner: Can I use the internet for my essay?
Teacher response: You could do.
Alternative teacher response:

Activity 9.6

Paying attention to the tone of your written responses

You can convey more than just the intended meaning of words when giving feedback. This activity asks you to improve some written feedback where the tone of the language could have a negative impact that will interfere with how the content will be received by the recipient.

Here is a teacher's written feedback on an undergraduate essay in education studies.

How would you rewrite the feedback, retaining the substance, but changing the words in order to have a less negative impact on the recipient?

The main problem with this essay is that you are less than clear about the distinction between behaviourism and constructivism. You have identified some of the differences (as I've noted in your text) but I'm not convinced you truly grasp what they are fundamentally about. I suppose that the course outline you suggest does embody a constructivist approach but you need to spell out the connections between theory and practice more. A lot of the problems stem from your clumsy phraseology – again I've noted (some) examples in the text – and what is either a faulty spellchecker or lack of proofreading. Only the first two arguments you offer have any bearing on the applicability of these theories in HE; the remaining three are not relevant. This is surprising in light of the amount of reading your references suggest you have done. The reference to Ramsden has the wrong date.

Chapter 10

Developing self-awareness as a teacher

This chapter includes the following activities:

What does it mean and why does it matter?

This chapter differs from the preceding chapters in that it does not suggest strategies for use with learners. Instead, it focuses on the process of you becoming more self-aware as a teacher. Self-awareness is at the heart of being emotionally intelligent and is a prerequisite for making sure that the strategies suggested in earlier chapters are successful.

Daniel Goleman defines it as 'knowing what we are feeling in the moment, and using those preferences to guide our decision making; having a realistic assessment of our own abilities and a well-grounded sense of self-confidence' (Goleman 1998: 318). I suggest three levels on which it is useful to develop self-awareness as a teacher. These are:

1.   awareness of your feelings at any one moment in relation to teaching;
2.   awareness of your values and attitudes as a teacher;
3.   awareness of your behaviours as a teacher and how others see them.

First, being aware of your feelings at any one time is especially significant for using emotional intelligence in your teaching. You cannot begin to tune into the feelings of others until you can tune into your own. Your ability to empathize and to accept how others feel depends, first of all, on how far you can know and accept yourself and your feelings. Even if you are accustomed to recognizing and articulating your feelings you may think that your self-awareness is not relevant to your work as a teacher. Yet, awareness of your feelings as a teacher is a prerequisite not just for using emotional intelligence in the classroom, but also for your own learning and development. Teachers are encouraged to learn through reflection, to become reflective practitioners. Attending to your feelings is an essential component of the process of engaging in successful reflective learning (see page 151).

Secondly, you need to be aware of your character, in particular your values and attitudes. The view of teaching adopted in this book lays great emphasis on the relationship between you and your learners. This was touched upon most obviously in Chapter 2. But how you relate to your learners is just one aspect of how you relate to others generally. Being effective as a teacher entails you 'knowing' your students to some extent, but you cannot 'know' others until you have begun to know yourself. Parker J. Palmer writes eloquently on the importance of self-knowledge as a teacher. It is the theme of his book, *The Courage to Teach*. He says, 'the more familiar we become with our inner terrain, the more surefooted our teaching – and living – becomes' (Palmer 2007: 6). He asserts, 'knowing myself is as crucial to good teaching as knowing my students and my subject' (ibid.: 3). This view is endorsed by Patricia Owen-Smith:

> If we as teachers are privileging the affective in our classrooms, we must know our own hearts and be willing to navigate our own inner landscape … the task of rescuing the affective in our students is even more difficult if we have not yet rescued our own hearts.
>
> (Owen-Smith 2008: 3)

The third significant strand of self-awareness is more tangible than the other two, as it concerns your visible behaviours. This includes your mannerisms, habits, the way you talk, your non-verbal communication and so on. In other words, all those things others can see and hear and that you may be aware of to a greater or lesser extent. This awareness is important, because if you are seeking to influence your learners' readiness to learn and their learning state, you will want to know how they perceive you and what effect this has on them. I met a teacher who gave the incomplete sentences from activity 10.2 below to her learners and asked them to complete the sentences about her. The responses showed that some of her learners perceived her as 'scary', which was at odds with how she perceived herself and not what she thought was helpful for their learning. As a result, she set out to change their perception.

Some teachers express an objection to the idea of emphasizing self-awareness in their work. They feel that it is inappropriate and can turn into an unhealthy self-obsession. It is true that while it is necessary to enquire about yourself, you must take care not to lose sight of the purpose of the enquiry. It is important to do it in order to understand yourself and how you relate to others and so be better able to improve those relationships. You need to ensure that it does not become indulgent, failing to lead to any productive change.

To develop self-awareness of your feelings can be a tough task. It requires honesty on your part. There is a tendency to focus on how you think you should be feeling, the kind of character you think you ought to be, and to block out emotions and characteristics which you find less acceptable. Indeed, Joanna Crossman suggests, 'teachers will need to take some personal risks in giving thought to who they are and the way they do what they do when interacting with learners in the classroom' (Crossman 2007: 325).

What is required is a 'non-reactive, non-judgemental attention to inner states' (Goleman 1996: 47). Being able to recognize, label and accept your feelings provides the basis for moving on to discuss and understand feelings. Key things to remember in becoming aware of your feelings are:

- be as truthful to yourself as you can;
- initially, do not rush to explain or justify, just focus on expressing and recognizing the feelings;
- find a suitable time and place for this exploration – you might choose to call on a supportive friend;
- if you can, accept what you discover about yourself, without leaping to judge it.

This process is not something that comes automatically to everyone. The culture you grew up in and, in particular, family expectations will have a great influence on the extent to which you are ready for this kind of self-awareness. For instance, if you come from a family where it was seen as a sign of weakness to express feelings, you may not be ready to recognize that you have feelings, let alone to articulate them and work with them.

When you start to develop awareness of yourself at the other levels – your values and attitudes and your behaviours – hopefully the process of discovery should not be so challenging. Nonetheless, it may still prove difficult to accept what you discover.

This chapter and the next four chapters are about aspects of self-awareness. The first four activities ask very specific questions to help you find out more about your character and behaviour. The final activity suggests a simple framework for expanding your degree of self-awareness.

This aspect of professional development differs from the conventional in two ways. First, it is never-ending. The quest for self-knowledge is perpetual because the self that you are is always shifting – it is not fixed. Carl Rogers's classic work, *On Becoming a Person*, was titled thus because he saw us as always in a state of 'becoming'. The activities in this chapter are intended as examples of the process of developing self-awareness. Secondly, this involves development of you as a person. It is not possible to separate the person at work from the person at home and elsewhere. Although the focus for the activities is work, the outcomes of developing self-awareness cannot be confined to the workplace.

Investigating your practice

Activity 10.1

Your stroking pattern

Like 'personal styles' in activities 2.3 and 9.3, the concept of 'strokes' (referred to earlier in Chapter 6) has its origins in Transactional Analysis (TA). A stroke is a 'unit of recognition' (Stewart and Joines 1987: 72), meaning anything you do, verbally or non-verbally, to acknowledge the existence of another: that is, speaking to someone or communicating with them by, for instance, a nod, a smile or even a frown. We all need strokes of some kind to survive, and we do tend to seek out certain kinds of stroke and sometimes to reject others that are offered. Equally, of course, we have the opportunity to give or to withhold strokes from others. This activity helps you to begin to compile a stroking pattern for yourself as a teacher. You can then consider changing your pattern, if it is not conducive to good teaching and a positive emotional environment.

This is a way to record your stroking pattern with a group of learners:

A positive stroke invites the person to whom it is offered to feel 'OK' about themselves and others. For example, 'That is a very useful question you have just asked.'

A negative stroke invites the person to whom it is offered to feel 'not OK' about themselves and others. For example, 'Don't ask such stupid questions!' When an opportunity arises for you to give a stroke, you can give it or refuse to give it, i.e. withhold it.

For this activity, you need to monitor, during a teaching session, the kind of strokes you give or withhold. After the session, complete the questionnaire below.

---

1. **When I had the opportunity to give a positive stroke, how often did I give one?**

   never   ☐
   seldom   ☐
   moderately   ☐
   often   ☐
   incessantly   ☐

   Examples:

2. **When I had the opportunity to give a positive stroke, how often did I withhold it?**

never   ☐
seldom   ☐
moderately   ☐
often   ☐
incessantly   ☐

Examples:

3. **When I had the opportunity to give a negative stroke, how often did I give one?**

never   ☐
seldom   ☐
moderately   ☐
often   ☐
incessantly   ☐

Examples:

4. **When I had the opportunity to give a negative stroke, how often did I withhold it?**

never   ☐
seldom   ☐
moderately   ☐
often   ☐
incessantly   ☐

Examples:

When someone else gives you a stroke, you can accept it or you can discount it. For instance, a learner says to you,

> *'The material on that handout is very clearly laid out.'*

You can accept – *Thank you.* Or you can discount:

> *Oh, it was the software I used; it does everything for me.*

Look back at your session again. Remember examples of strokes being given to you, and for each one, ask:

- Was it positive or negative?
- Did I accept it or discount it?

You have now begun to build up your stroking pattern, which shows how you give and withhold, accept and discount strokes, both positive and negative. This pattern can affect your relationships with others. For example, if you continually discount positive strokes offered, others may cease to try to offer them, anticipating your response.

Consider whether you would like to change your pattern. For example, you may want to reduce the number of negative strokes you give, or accept more of the positive strokes you are offered. Normally if you succeed in changing one part of your stroking pattern it will have an effect on another. If you put more energy into giving positive strokes, you will spend less time giving negative ones.

Record which part(s) of your pattern you plan to change and how: for example, 'I plan to accept more of the positive strokes I am offered.'

Activity 10.2

Knowing yourself as a teacher

This activity invites you to consider how others see you as a teacher. While the task may appear straightforward, you may find some of the sentences difficult to complete.

Complete the following sentences in relation to yourself as a teacher:

My most common mannerism is

The phrase I most commonly use is

Learners are most likely to leave my session feeling

My greatest skill as a teacher is

A skill as a teacher that I could handle better is

The quality I display that learners respond to best is

I respond best to learners who

If there is one thing I do too much of, it is

If there is one thing I could do more of, it is

Learners find my manner predominantly

If you have the opportunity, consider asking a colleague or a group of learners whom you know particularly well whether they have five minutes to complete these sentences in relation to you as a teacher. Comparing your perception with theirs can be very helpful in developing self-awareness.

Activity 10.3

What shapes your values and attitudes in teaching?

Part of the make-up of our character as a teacher is our set of values and attitudes. These are not necessarily fixed, and one way to get more in tune with ourselves is to clarify what these values are, and then to look at where they originated and how they have changed.

Here are 12 characteristics that can be associated with teachers. Rank them 1–12 in order of importance to you.

Characteristic	Ranking 1–12
Expertise	☐
Warmth	☐
Enthusiasm	☐
Flexibility	☐
Dynamism	☐
Patience	☐
Attentiveness	☐
Sense of humour	☐
Reliability	☐
Perseverance	☐
Readiness to experiment	☐
Ability to improvise	☐

What makes you grade them in this order? For instance, is it your own experience as a learner, long ago or recently? Or is it your experience as a teacher?

How much would your ranking have been different if you had done this exercise 5 years ago, or perhaps 10 years ago?

Why is that?

Activity 10.4

Drivers

The concept of 'drivers' is another that has its origins in Transactional Analysis (see Chapter 2). It suggests that on occasion we are unconsciously acting in response to messages we picked up in early childhood. For instance, we may have understood from our parents or whoever was significant in our upbringing that we were 'OK' as long as we hurried up. Because of this we engage in 'Hurry Up' behaviours, often without being aware of it. We are *driven* to 'Hurry Up', and do so indiscriminately, which means that we display both the positive sides and the drawbacks of 'Hurry Up' behaviours. If we could develop awareness of this we might be able to control our drive to 'Hurry Up', recognizing that it does not always result in appropriate behaviours but that on occasion it gives us some strengths that can be useful. This applies as much in the teaching context as in any other.

There are five such drivers:

1. Be Perfect
2. Please Others
3. Try Hard
4. Be Strong
5. Hurry Up.

Here are some characteristics of each driver:

Be Perfect
Pays attention to detail, well organized; prepares thoroughly; presents written work well; can lose sight of the big picture; can miss deadlines in the pursuit of perfection; can be seen as irritating.

Please Others
Good team member; empathic; looks for harmony; supportive of others; reluctant to challenge; does not invite respect; can take on too much work through not saying no.

Try Hard
Enthusiastic; thorough; energetic; likely to lose interest too soon; can make too much of a small task.

Be Strong
Calm; reliable; dutiful; good under pressure; doesn't ask for help and gets overloaded; hard to get to know well.

Hurry Up
Gets through a lot of work; efficient; good at short deadlines; makes mistakes in haste; can be seen to be impatient.

For each statement below, consider it in relation to you as a teacher and decide whether you agree, agree to some extent or disagree.

	agree	agree to some extent	disagree
1. I pay great attention to organizing the room efficiently	☐	☐	☐
2. I often wait until as late as possible to prepare	☐	☐	☐
3. I am described as calm, balanced and even-tempered	☐	☐	☐
4. I enjoy encouraging learners and doing things to help	☐	☐	☐
5. I sometimes overload learners with information	☐	☐	☐
6. I feel it is important to be liked	☐	☐	☐
7. I usually work from outline notes only	☐	☐	☐
8. I am aware that my explanations sometimes go off at a tangent	☐	☐	☐
9. I am very quick in my preparation	☐	☐	☐
10. I tend to include everything there is to know about the subject	☐	☐	☐
11. I feel I am intuitive and sensitive to others' feelings	☐	☐	☐
12. I plan ahead thoroughly and am ready for any problems that might arise	☐	☐	☐
13. I often expect learners to do far more than is possible in the time	☐	☐	☐
14. I tend to hide or control my feelings	☐	☐	☐
15. I dislike conflict	☐	☐	☐
16. I am good at getting new things off the ground	☐	☐	☐

	agree	agree to some extent	disagree
17. I know I am sometimes seen as aloof and unapproachable	☐	☐	☐
18. I enjoy explaining precisely and in detail	☐	☐	☐
19. I often turn up just in time	☐	☐	☐
20. I can tend to make tasks too big for learners	☐	☐	☐
21. I can have a problem saying 'no', even when I have not got the time	☐	☐	☐
22. I prefer not to ask for help and to do it alone	☐	☐	☐
23. I am certain there will be no mistakes in my materials	☐	☐	☐
24. I am happy to be depended on	☐	☐	☐
25. I can go fairly rapidly from enthusiasm to boredom	☐	☐	☐

Score one point for each 'agree' answer and a half point for each 'agree to some extent' answer. Find out how many points you have under each of the five categories below.

If your score is 3 or more for any category, this may be a significant driver for you.

						Total
Be Perfect statements:	1	5	12	18	23	
Please Others statements:	4	6	11	15	21	
Try Hard statements:	8	10	16	20	25	
Be Strong statements:	3	14	17	22	24	
Hurry Up statements:	2	7	9	13	19	

The key question is whether you exert control over when you exhibit the behaviours associated with the driver. In other words, do you engage in, say, 'Please Others' behaviours when it is useful and appropriate, or just compulsively and indiscriminately? Each driver has positive aspects but each can be counter-productive if followed to excess. Consider how you might exercise more control over your driver behaviours to make the most of your years of practice in that area. You can read more on drivers in *TA Today* by Ian Stewart and Vann Joines on pages 155–69 or, under the alternative description of 'working styles', in *Transactional Analysis for Trainers* by Julie Hay.

Developing your practice

Activity 10.5

Increasing the flow of information about yourself

You can improve communication by increasing the amount of information about yourself that is deliberately exchanged between you and your learners.

This activity asks you to explore the unknown parts of yourself – that is, the parts that you are aware of but that are unknown to others and the parts that others know of but that are unknown to you. It is a starting point for planning for more open communication in the following ways:

- offering information about your behaviours, thoughts, feelings and values to learners so that they have a fuller picture of you and less room for misinterpreting you;
- seeking feedback from learners about yourself so that you can have a fuller picture of yourself.

1. List things about yourself that are known to you but not to your learners. These might include interests, background, the area you live in, feelings about a session, your views on the session topic, your current working situation.
2. Choose from the list one or more items that you would feel comfortable revealing to a group of learners, and which would not feel inappropriate to reveal.
3. Plan for how you will reveal it or them to the group.
4. Now consider what aspects of yourself might be known to learners but not to you – what they pick up about you from what they see and hear of you.
5. Plan for a way to ask for some feedback on this from learners. You could draw on the lists in activities 10.2 or 18.6. Or you could, for instance, include a question like this on your feedback sheet:
    'In what aspects of presentation could the teacher improve?'
    You might need to make it known that comments on any aspect will be welcome, as long as they are intended constructively.

Chapter 11

Recognizing your prejudices and preferences

This chapter includes the following activities:

11.1   First impressions
11.2   Your prejudices and preferences

What does it mean and why does it matter?

Self-awareness is an integral part of emotional intelligence, and one of the most difficult aspects of developing self-awareness is to confront your prejudices. The swift reaction of most teachers when asked whether they have any prejudices towards others would be to say that they treat all equally. However, it is impossible to be unbiased, and we are all tempted to categorize others. This can be on the basis of gender, accent, age, appearance and so on. Prejudices distort our understanding of others. To assume a set of characteristics based on one factor means that you will be less able to read accurately who that person is. In addition to these assumed characteristics that derive from prejudice, you may have quite legitimate preferences in terms of which types of learner you prefer to work with. For example, you may have preferences for learners when you perceive that their values or attitudes match your own.

Imagine that you have two new groups of learners for the same subject. The first group comprises people in the age range 35 to 50 and the second consists of 16/17-year-olds. You need to ask yourself:

- Will you treat them differently in any way? If your answer is yes, in what way?
- What are your reasons for treating them differently?
- Most importantly, what evidence justifies treating them differently?
- How reliable is that evidence?

If you do tend to treat some 'types' of learner differently from others, it is always worth scrutinizing the validity of your reasons for doing so.

As a teacher, if you treat learners differently on the basis of these preferences and prejudices, you will be assuming different learning characteristics or abilities.

You will invariably find evidence to support your assumptions, whether they are right or wrong. For instance, if you have an older learner and assume they will experience some difficulty, you are likely to interpret responses they make in terms of difficulty when you would treat the same responses from another learner differently. In addition, your behaviour towards the learners can affect them in such a way as to reinforce your assumptions, so that you may actually unconsciously encourage them to experience difficulty. Your perception becomes a self-fulfilling prophecy. The 'halo' effect reinforces the initial positive impression you have of someone, while the 'reverse halo' effect reinforces your original negative impression. You will also influence the way that learner responds to you.

You may find that you put more energy into your responses to certain learners because they have triggered a feeling in you, positive or negative, that is not related to their ability or their readiness to learn. For example, I have seen a teacher respond strongly after inferring that a particular learner had a political viewpoint opposed to theirs. The teacher devoted a great deal of time to negating what that learner had to offer. There was no direct connection between the subject being taught and politics. The teacher's response was not helpful for that learner nor for the rest of the group. This was an example of the strong feelings of the teacher overriding their fairness and effectiveness.

So the emotionally intelligent approach begins by seeking to become aware of your prejudices. Then you may be better equipped to spot the learners who are likely to provoke strong responses in you, favourable or unfavourable. Once you recognize that you may be contributing to unhelpful interactions, that will hopefully give you the motivation to review and change your way of communicating in order to avoid similar problems in the future.

Investigating your practice

Activity 11.1

First impressions

A group whom you have not met before is assembling for the session. As you look around, you see that amongst the group are these five people:

- younger female, quizzical, stern;
- older male, arms crossed, looking irritable;
- younger male, looking tired, slumped;
- older female, looking agitated and tense;
- older female, smiling, upright, attentive.

Picture each of them in turn and for each one, answer these questions:

1. What feelings does the person's appearance arouse in you?
2. What word best describes the behaviour you anticipate from this person as a learner?
3. What must you say to yourself to ensure you do not let your immediate impressions override your effectiveness as a teacher?
4. What strategies can you adopt to ensure this?

Activity 11.2

Your prejudices and preferences

Under each heading below, finish the incomplete sentence and then answer the questions that follow, in order to begin to explore your prejudices and preferences in relation to learners.

Appearance of learners

I pay more attention to learners whose appearance is . . .

1. Why is that?

2. What is behind your answer to 1? Probe a little deeper.

3. What effect do you think this has on the learner?

4. What effect do you think this has on the other learners?

5. What influence does this have on your effectiveness as a teacher?

Behaviour of learners

I pay more attention to learners whose behaviour is . . .

1. Why is that?

2. What is behind your answer to 1? Probe a little deeper.

3. What effect do you think this has on the learner?

4. What effect do you think this has on the other learners?

5. What influence does this have on your effectiveness as a teacher?

Attitudes of learners

I pay more attention to learners whose attitude is . . .

1. Why is that?

2. What is behind your answer to 1? Probe a little deeper.

3. What effect do you think this has on the learner?

4. What effect do you think this has on the other learners?

5. What influence does this have on your effectiveness as a teacher?

Developing your practice

The two activities in this chapter have introduced you to the initial steps you need to take in dealing with the effects of your prejudices and preferences as a teacher. They are:

1. Become aware of your prejudices and preferences.
2. Identify exactly how they might distort your ability to understand others and to help them learn.

The two steps you must then take are:

3. Make a conscious decision to set your prejudices and preferences aside.
4. If that is not possible, consciously try to minimize or eradicate their influence on your teaching.

You may find it useful to monitor your responses in a particular session. Do you find that you are paying more or less attention to some learners than to others? If so, what is the cause of that? Is it because of assumptions you are making based on one factor, for example age or gender? Plan for specific behaviours in future which will help you eradicate this bias. For example, you might resolve in the next session with this group to speak first to the person you have been ignoring this time. This type of activity is well suited to the format of the reflective diary as outlined in Activity 18.5.

Chapter 12

Your non-verbal communication

This chapter includes the following activities:

12.1   Reflecting on your non-verbal communication
12.2   Experimenting with your posture

What does it mean and why does it matter?

One potent way in which you communicate with your learners is through non-verbal communication. This includes your facial expressions, your posture, what you do with your arms, hands and so on. It also includes the sound of your voice. To teach with emotional intelligence demands an awareness of your non-verbal communication, as this can influence how your learners are feeling. Unfortunately, all too often we are unaware of exactly what we are communicating. For learners, too, the effect of your non-verbal communication may be unconscious, but that doesn't make it any the less significant.

Everyone is accustomed to reading non-verbal communication at some level, even if they are doing it unconsciously. Appearance and non-verbal communication are often all you have to go on when you first meet someone new, which makes those first few minutes very important. If you form an initial impression of someone based on their non-verbal communication, you may be inclined to interpret what they say or do afterwards in those terms. Even if your learners' reading of your non-verbal communication is inaccurate, it is still important because it influences their response and behaviour. If the non-verbal communication message you are giving is at odds with what you are saying, the non-verbal message is likely to be perceived as more trustworthy.

Your non-verbal communication is sending messages to learners and is influencing their response to you and to the session – it is another aspect of your communication which cannot fail to have an effect. The implication of this is quite alarming. For example, you have prepared a brilliant talk or lecture that draws on your expert knowledge and uses an excellent set of slides but your non-verbal communication, which says you are impatient, or anxious and distracted, is what your learners will register most strongly.

Of course, you cannot determine the effect your non-verbal communication is going to have on learners. For example, you may fold your arms across your chest because you feel more comfortable or because you are cold. However, it will still convey to some learners that you are being defensive. Any cultural differences between you and the students will also play a large part. For example, your smile may have alternative interpretations among the group of learners, depending on each individual's cultural influences.

Consider the following few examples of non-verbal communication and ask how far you think you are already aware of them when you teach. Which of them do you do, and how frequently?

- Hands clasped in front of you
- Playing with a ring on your finger
- Fiddling with an object, e.g. flip-chart marker
- Adjusting your glasses
- Pushing you hair back.

Non-verbal communication extends to your facial expressions. We all have a natural facial expression – do you know what yours is? Whenever I look at a group of learners, for example, there will be that mix of bright, cheery, welcoming faces and others that are just glum. One potential problem is when your expression is not congruent with your mood. Most importantly, if your natural expression is, for example, miserable, even when you feel at one with the world, those on the receiving end of your stare will see 'miserable' and, unless they know you quite well, will respond appropriately to this apparent expression of feeling. The same applies to the tone and expression of your voice. Can you say, for instance, whether yours is light or heavy, hesitant or urgent, harsh or soft?

Have you ever thought what you would want your non-verbal communication to be conveying to your learners? Do you want to come across as:

- confident?
- authoritative?
- open?
- approachable?
- enthusiastic?
- all of the above?

Does your current non-verbal communication convey this? Too often we are not sending out the message we would like to. Our real feelings 'leak' out and learners can pick up on our uncertainty, anxiety, impatience and all of those other feelings that we may not want to be known or, indeed, even be aware of ourselves.

It is reasonable at this point to object and say, 'I would prefer my non-verbal communication to be natural, not false.' Becoming too self-aware will be counter-productive, but just as you exercise some control over what you say verbally to a group, so you should be alert to the non-verbal communication you are using. The goal is to strike a balance between being disciplined about your non-verbal communication, exercising some control over it while, at the same time, being natural.

The activities that follow are intended to help you address the key questions about non-verbal communication:

- Do I know what my non-verbal communication is like?
- Can I guess at its impact?
- What impact would I like it to have?
- Would I like to modify it and, if so, in what way?
- How will I achieve that?

Investigating your practice

Activity 12.1

Reflecting on your non-verbal communication

You can never really know how others see you, but a video recording can be a very useful device for getting some idea of what others see. This activity suggests how you can make the most of even a brief recording of you with a group of learners. Of course, if you do make a recording you will need to check with your learners that it is OK to do so if they are included, and to reassure them of its purpose and that they are in no way being observed or assessed themselves.

Step 1

Make a video recording of yourself teaching for at least ten minutes.

Step 2

As soon as possible after making the recording, watch it with the sound turned down. For each of the six items in the list that follows, answer these three questions:

- What do you observe?
- What does that say about what you were thinking at that time?
- What effect does this have on your audience?

1. Where your gaze is directed
2. What you do with your hands
3. Your posture

4.   Your facial expression
5.   How, where and how often you move
6.   Any noticeable physical traits.

Step 3

Now watch the recording again with the sound turned up. Try to ignore the content of what you are saying and listen to the tone and intonation of your voice as though you had never heard it before. Describe it.

Step 4

Consider these questions:

•   How much control are you exerting over these components of non-verbal communication?
•   Is there any mismatch between your verbal and non-verbal communication?
•   Is your non-verbal communication helping you to convey the impression you would like to convey to your learners?
•   Should you attempt to change or modify any aspect of your non-verbal communication?

Activity 12.2

Experimenting with your posture

Here are descriptions of eight different postures that a teacher could adopt in front of a group of learners.

1.   Seated (not behind a table) and leaning forward
2.   Seated (not behind a table) and relaxed to the point of slouching
3.   Seated (not behind a table) with arms folded
4.   Standing, hands on hips
5.   Standing, hands clasped in front
6.   Standing, arms outstretched and welcoming
7.   Seated, behind a table
8.   Standing, behind a table, arms straight, hands on table.

For each one of the above:

•   Try this posture now while imagining a group in front of you.
•   Does the posture feel deliberate or natural?
•   How else can you describe how it feels?
•   Do you use this posture?

- How do you think learners might perceive you in this posture (for example, authoritative; threatening; confident; welcoming)?

Developing your practice

The first step in developing your practice in non-verbal communication is to become aware of what you currently do. The activities above and some of the questions earlier in the chapter should have helped you to start on this. The next step is to plan how you can make changes to your non-verbal communication. One way is to resolve to change a particular aspect: for example, to adopt a new posture when welcoming a group or to make sure you never fiddle distractedly with your pen while talking to a group. Secondly, you can plan for how you are going to monitor your non-verbal communication in a session. For example, decide that every time a learner asks a question, as well as paying attention to it and responding you will ask yourself, 'What is my non-verbal communication at this point and what message is it conveying to the learner?'

Chapter 13

Shaping and handling your feelings

This chapter includes the following activities:

13.1 Checking your mindset
13.2 Adopting realistic beliefs
13.3 Learned optimism
13.4 Recognizing and handling strong feelings in the moment
13.5 Reflecting on how you handled strong feelings

What does it mean and why does it matter?

Much of this book is directly concerned with how you, as a teacher, handle and influence the feelings of your learners. However, your own feelings as a teacher deserve equal attention. There is no doubt that you can experience some very strong and occasionally very conflicting feelings while teaching. For example: 'I remember feeling a sense of rising panic . . . I felt very vulnerable . . . sweat was beginning to seep through my shirt' (Gilbert 2004: 34). The teacher quoted here is new to his job, but strong feelings do not necessarily diminish as you get older and more experienced. Teacher and author Parker J. Palmer, with 25 years' experience, encountered a learner who he described as 'The Student from Hell' and, in his own judgement, did not handle the situation well. He writes, 'I left that class with a powerful combination of feelings: self-pity, fraudulence and rage' (Palmer 2007: 46).

While your normal teaching experience is unlikely to provide you with such an overwhelming depth of emotional response, you should be concerned if you do not experience strong feelings from time to time. These may be feelings you will welcome, such as exhilaration, relief and joy. Handling strong feelings such as these need not be problematic. It is the other troubling feelings, when you are outraged, shocked, insulted, offended, disappointed or frustrated, that pose more of a threat to the well-being of you and your learners as well as a threat to achieving the goals of the session.

Take a moment to recall times when you have experienced strong feelings while teaching. What kinds of feelings do you recall?

The techniques for developing self-awareness (see Chapter 10) are important for ensuring you are able, first, to identify these feelings. Once you have acknowledged the feelings you experience as a teacher, you may be tempted to take one of two opposing but extreme steps, both of which are unhealthy and not emotionally intelligent.

One is to suppress your feelings, to deny their importance or just pretend they are not there. This can lead to more stress for you and poor relationships with others if you are withholding your feelings from them. In doing this, you are not showing respect for yourself and it makes it almost impossible for you to accept others who do express their feelings. The other extreme is to blurt it all out in every detail and let everybody know how you are feeling all of the time, which is overwhelming for the recipient, indulgent on your part and unprofessional.

A more useful response is to engage in self-regulation. This is described by Geetu Bharwaney as 'being able to face disruptive emotions like anger and fear and making choices when you are in the middle of a crisis' (Bharwaney 2007: 16). Self-regulation involves judicious choice on your part about what is the appropriate thing to say and do, given the feelings aroused in you, the context you are in and what your goals are in that context.

However, there is much you can do to make it less likely that you will have overwhelming, unproductive feelings to contend with. Activities 13.1 and 13.2 suggest strategies for this, whilst activity 13.3 draws on the same principles and offers a strategy for determining feelings in the face of adversity. Activity 13.4 gives you the chance to anticipate a challenging situation and rehearse how you might respond. You can never be sure on any occasion that you will say and do just the right thing, and you also need to ensure that you deal with those episodes that were challenging, after the event, so activity 13.5 gives you the chance to reflect on one or more incidents and see whether you can learn from them.

Activities 13.4 and 13.5 are particularly suitable for completing with the assistance of someone else who can help you reflect on your responses (see, for example, activities 18.2 and 18.5 in Chapter 18).

The key points about shaping and handling your feelings are:

- recognize your feelings;
- consider the way in which your thoughts can determine your feelings and whether you want to change your thoughts and what opportunities you have to do so;
- handle your feelings in order to look after the interests of both you and your learners;
- make sure you take time to talk through, reflect on, and hopefully learn from your experiences of handling feelings.

Investigating your practice

Activity 13.1

Checking your mindset

By 'mindset', in relation to a teaching session, I mean the view of the session, and in particular of the learners, that you take in there with you. This might be, even unconsciously, in the form of a metaphor such as those in activity 2.1 above. For example, if you approach the session with the metaphor that sees you as a 'law enforcer to the potentially criminal', this will affect how you feel – wary, defensive, suspicious. You will be looking for confirmation of your mindset and you will be likely to provoke behaviour and responses in learners that will give you that confirmation. In other words, your thoughts affect your feelings, which affect your behaviour, which in turn influences the response of the group. The 'law enforcer' will have a different experience from the 'gardener', although the group is the same.

I heard a story of a woman who did not work in education but had to do a lot of presentations in her job. When asked to identify her mindset in anticipation of a presentation, she said that she saw herself as 'on trial', and anticipating a guilty verdict. She was persuaded and helped to adopt a different mindset of 'about to share some useful information with friends'. Once she was able to adopt this, she became more confident and began to develop her skills and to enjoy her presentations, which were more successful.

So the first step is to be aware of the mindset you may be unconsciously taking into the session. Review it and ask yourself whether it is going to help you and your learners. If not, select an alternative that will be more helpful and work on installing that new one.

The principle can also be applied to incidents that arise during a session.

How do you view the following?

1. blank faces and a low level of interaction by learners
    I view this as . . .
    (for example, as an irritation? as an indication of their lack of ability?)

2.   an irrelevant question from a learner
     I view this as . . .

3.   conflict between learners
     I view this as . . .

4.   a learner's statement that they are overwhelmed and confused
     I view this as . . .

5.   a learner's challenging question to you
     I view this as . . .

Here are some potentially productive views you could adopt of each of the above. In each case, consider what you might do or say if you adopted that view.

1. If I viewed blank faces and a low level of interaction from the learners as an invitation for me to seek feedback on their understanding, I would demonstrate this by:

2. If I viewed an irrelevant question as an opportunity for me to provide clarification to the learner, I would demonstrate this by:

3. If I viewed conflict between learners as an opportunity for them to find out more about each other's perspective, I would demonstrate this by:

4. If I viewed a learner's statement that they are overwhelmed and confused as an opportunity for me to find out more, I would demonstrate this by:

5. If I viewed a learner's challenging question to me as a chance for greater learning, I would demonstrate this by:

Activity 13.2

Adopting realistic beliefs

Another way in which thoughts can influence feelings is through rigid unrealistic beliefs that you hold. For instance, you may believe that:

'All learners ought to do work in between sessions.'

When you discover that some learners have not, you may feel exasperated, frustrated and so on. If you adopt a more realistic belief such as:

'It's really important for learners to do work in between sessions but I recognize that some learners are unlikely ever to do this,'

you are less likely to be overwhelmed by such feelings, as your belief is more closely matched to reality.

To make your beliefs more realistic does not mean that you lower your standards and, for example, say that not doing work in between sessions is acceptable behaviour or excusable or satisfactory; you will still make this clear to learners. It means only that when work is not done, you are less vulnerable to unwanted feelings that reduce your ability to function effectively.

In the grid below, see whether you can identify an unrealistic thought or belief of yours from the left-hand column, and speculate on how you could replace it with a more realistic one such as in the right-hand column.

Unrealistic thoughts/beliefs	Realistic thoughts/beliefs
Learners should always turn up on time.	I think punctuality is essential, but I acknowledge there will probably always be some learners who will not be on time.
Learners should attend all lectures.	I would prefer full attendance at all lectures, but I recognize that that is unlikely to happen.
My learners ought to be interested in all of the course, not just what is likely to be assessed.	I would like learners to be less instrumental in what parts of the course they focus on, but I realize that for some learners, assessment is all that counts.
Learners must recognize that success only comes with effort.	I have no doubt that effort is necessary to success, yet I also acknowledge that not all learners think the same way.
Learners ought to be ready to join in, to participate fully in sessions.	I think it is a student's responsibility to participate fully in classes, but I recognize there will always be some learners who think differently.

Activity 13.3

Learned optimism

Martin Seligman proposes the concept of 'learned optimism' for use in harnessing the power of your feelings to help you deal with adversity and achieve your goals. It is about how you talk to yourself when you experience adversity and the feelings that result. You can develop your use of optimism using Seligman's ABCDE model. Here's an example of how it might apply during a teaching session where you have tried out a new activity with your learners and it has not gone well:

> A is for **adversity** – the thing that did not go well, the setback, in this case the failed activity.
> B is for **belief** – this means what you said to yourself in response to the adversity; in other words, your interpretation of the episode. You might have said, 'Clearly this has failed. I should never have tried it in the first place, it was a bad idea.' You might continue, '. . . and is another example of why I am just not cut out for teaching'.
> C is for **consequence**, that is, the feelings that result from what you said to yourself in 'B'. In this case you might feel frustrated, inadequate, dejected.
> D is for **disputation**, where you stand back and look again at what you said in 'B'. You take a more considered, objective view. You might say to yourself, 'In fact, the principles behind the activity were sound. The rest of the session has gone well and those 10 minutes on that activity could have gone better, but they were not wasted and it has not affected the learners' engagement.'
> E is for **energisation**. This is how you feel after disputing your original interpretation, that is, more ready to continue and not dragged down by the unproductive feelings you experienced at point C.

Select a setback you have experienced, and see whether the ABCDE sequence would apply.

This model acknowledges the power of feelings in enabling or hindering our ability to progress and deal with what's next, in this case continuing with a teaching session. It is also based on the idea that feelings are often determined by thoughts or beliefs or interpretations. So monitoring and perhaps modifying our thoughts can affect how we feel, which in turn can leave us better prepared. Seligman says that 'becoming an optimist consists . . . simply of learning a set of skills about how to talk to *yourself* when you suffer a personal defeat' (Seligman 2006: 207). He suggests we should be ready, when encountering adversity, to listen to our internal dialogue and, if it is pessimistic, be ready to dispute it.

Pessimists typically use interpretations that are:

- Permanent   'The effects of this setback are long-lasting.'
- Pervasive   'The setback will affect everything.'

- Personal   'I am solely responsible for the setback.'

Seligman does not prescribe optimism as a solution on every occasion. Using optimism suits some situations and roles at work but not others, for instance, 'If the cost of failure is high, optimism is the wrong strategy' (ibid.: 209) Also, you cannot be justified in suggesting that every setback is not your responsibility. Furthermore, some element of pessimism is necessary and 'You can choose *not* to dispute the pessimistic thoughts' (ibid.: 292).

> What we want is not blind optimism but flexible optimism – optimism with its eyes open. We must be able to use pessimism's keen sense of reality when we need it, but without having to dwell in its dark shadows.
>
> (Ibid.: 292)

Knowing how to use optimism gives you a choice. 'If you learn optimism, you can choose to use its techniques whenever you need them – without becoming a slave to them' (ibid.: 291).

Activity 13.4

Recognizing and handling strong feelings in the moment

We've all had a comment or question from a learner that we have found very challenging. This activity guides you in working out the best response to your most demanding situation.

1. Think of something that a learner might say or do that would provoke strong feelings in you which could be overwhelming or hard to control. Write it down in the space below.

2. What would be your gut reaction to what the learner said or did – what would you be saying to yourself?

3. What would you *like* to say in response?

4. What words can you use to describe the feelings that would be aroused in you by what the learner said or did?

5. Go back to your gut reaction. What is it about what the learner said or did that triggers your reaction?

6. If you could make the perfect response to the learner, what would you want it to achieve:
    - for your benefit?
    - for the learner's benefit?
    - for the benefit of the rest of the group?

7. Taking account of what you would like your response to achieve, carefully word the perfect response.

Activity 13.5

Reflecting on how you handled strong feelings

This activity gives you the opportunity to review an occasion when you experienced strong feelings as a teacher, and equips you with a series of questions that you can use to be better prepared for such occasions in the future.

1. Select an incident with a group or learner in a group that aroused strong feelings in you.

2. Describe what happened. Don't make judgements yet or try to draw conclusions: simply describe. Make sure you include just facts – no inferences or assumptions.

3. Describe how you felt at the time.

4. What are the key words in articulating these feelings, for example angry, shocked, vulnerable? (It is worth also asking, 'Are they familiar?', 'Am I, deep down, comfortable with them?')

5. What was your outward reaction?

6. To what extent were you able to manage those feelings?

7. Looking back, what sense can you make of the incident and your reactions?

8. What conclusions can you draw from the incident and your reactions?

9. If the same thing happened tomorrow:
    *   would it provoke the same feelings in you?
    *   would you be able to manage the feelings it provoked?
    *   what would your outward reaction be?

10. Look back at all of your answers above. What have you learned from this exercise?

Developing your practice

Being prepared to deliberately attempt to shape your feelings by determining your thoughts, beliefs and interpretations ought to both make you less likely to be impeded by your feelings and enable you to harness the power of your feelings to make you feel more resourceful and confident.

To develop your skill at handling strong feelings while teaching, you need to take the opportunity to learn from such occasions as they arise. Activity 13.5 provides a framework, which you can use or modify, to help you reflect productively on these events. It is important not to underplay incidents that evoke strong responses in you, and also to set aside time to reflect on them in a structured way, if you are seeking to become more adept in this vital aspect of emotional intelligence.

Chapter 14

Revealing your feelings to learners

This chapter includes the following activities:

14.1   How far do you reveal your feelings to learners?
14.2   Planning to reveal your feelings to learners

What does it mean and why does it matter?

I once interviewed a teacher in further education about the impact on his work of a course he had done. The course was on counselling skills in education and training. One of his comments was: 'As a result of the course, I now see students as human beings.' He meant that he now saw beyond the particular categories that he or his institution had placed learners into, such as 'mature', 'first year' and so on, and was able to catch a glimpse of the individual behind the role of learner.

This comment by the teacher may be seen as a shift on his part to being more authentic in his teaching. Patricia Cranton and Ellen Carusetta suggest that new teachers are likely to draw on a 'teacher persona' as a guide for how they should behave in the classroom (Cranton and Carusetta 2004). That persona is based on role models from their time as students and from collectively held views about what a teacher should be. At the same time they 'rely on social norms to define *student* and then use these norms to form rules about how students behave' (ibid.: 291). While teachers have this blanket understanding of who the students are, it prevents them from seeing students as individuals and thereby from forming relationships with them. Changes come about through experience, through the questioning of these personae and from reflection on practice. In the case of the teacher quoted above, the course he had attended had clearly given him that opportunity to reflect on his practice and to adjust his views in a move to greater authenticity on his part.

How often do your learners see you as 'human'? How far are they aware of the person who inhabits the role of teacher? How far should they be aware? It is impossible to be emotionally intelligent in your teaching while hiding the person you are behind your role. Showing your learners that you are human too and that you have feelings is not only essential for your use of emotional intelligence, it also affects the emotional climate in the room and is the basis for a healthy relationship between you and them.

Of course, it is possible to misinterpret what this means in practice. It does not mean you should abuse your position to reveal all to your learners and use them as a captive audience for a series of revelations about your private life. Nor does it mean simply telling your learners when you feel exasperated about them and their behaviour. It does not mean you should encourage inappropriate relationships or topics for discussion in the classroom. If you are preparing your learners for a particular vocation, it would not help to model a way of behaving that would be unsuitable for their profession.

What it does mean is that there is room for some recognition by you and your learners of your feelings and your true personality. If there is to be emotional intelligence in the classroom, there must be recognition and acceptance of the emotional dimension in all of us. It is okay to reveal yourself as an emotional being and to transcend your role, showing that you are not simply the repository of skills and knowledge associated with your expertise and your profession.

As outlined earlier (Chapter 7), Carl Rogers (1961) advocated that one of the three qualities that a successful teacher should exhibit was *genuineness*. He sometimes used the term *transparency* or *congruence* instead. We might say *open*. By this he meant that you should not put on a façade and that you should be yourself with learners. This involves being ready to let your learners know how you feel, not by giving them minute-by-minute commentary on your feelings but rather doing so when it is appropriate. Indeed, a lack of authenticity will be difficult to sustain, as your real feelings are likely to 'leak' out. A number of learners' classroom activities ask them to reflect on their personal experience and it is questionable, as Bruce Macfarlane discusses (Macfarlane 2004: 121–6), to encourage them to be personal while you retain an emotional distance.

The two activities that follow are linked. Activity 14.1 invites you to consider whether and how far you reveal your feelings at the moment and, if so, which ones. Activity 14.2 invites you to think more about whether and when you should be revealing your feelings.

Investigating your practice

Activity 14.1

How far do you reveal your feelings to learners?

Making deliberate disclosures to groups of learners about how you are feeling can be a very potent device for encouraging them to see the person behind the role and for affecting the learning climate. Such actions need to be handled with care, and this activity comprises three steps in reviewing the kinds of feeling that you are already revealing to your learners.

Step 1

It is probable that there will be occasions when you draw on stories from your personal experience to assist your explanations to learners. Think of some of these stories. For each story, ask:

- Does it reveal feelings of yours?
- If so, what kinds of feeling of yours does it reveal? For example surprise, fear, joy, confusion?
- Is there any repetition of feelings conveyed? Are there any patterns?

Step 2

Below is a list of feelings that can be revealed in personal anecdotes. Take each feeling in turn and put them under one of the three headings in the table that follows. You may want to add other feelings to the columns.

anger; joy; grief; greed; happiness; relief; confusion; triumph; helplessness; worry; exhilaration; anxiety; elation; panic; terror; annoyance; boredom; concern; irritation; excitement; envy; despair; agitation; impatience

1	2	3
I have revealed this feeling to a group of learners	**I have not yet revealed this feeling to a group of learners but I could do so**	**I would never reveal this feeling to a group of learners**

Step 3

Take one of the feelings from column 3. Consider your reason for never revealing it to a group. Is it because:

- you want to control the image they have of you?
- you do not think it promotes a learning climate?
- you are not comfortable in yourself with having this feeling?
- or any other reason?

Repeat step 3 with as many feelings from column 3 as you wish.

Developing your practice

Activity 14.2

Planning to reveal your feelings to learners

Think of a session you will be running. Look at your entries in the columns in activity 14.1 above. Find a feeling from column 2, or perhaps column 3, that you could reveal to the group in a story which will illustrate the points you are making or explaining. Plan for how you will introduce and tell the story.

Chapter 15

Teaching with emotional intelligence one-to-one

The focus in the preceding chapters is largely on teachers working with groups of learners. Given that many teachers still have at least some work with individual learners, it is useful to explore to what extent these ideas of teaching with emotional intelligence apply when working one-to-one and whether they differ in that context.

Working one-to-one may have as its focus the learner's dissertation, project or portfolio, it may involve developing their academic skills or it may be personal tutoring. All of these roles have the intention of 'supporting, facilitating, enabling and empowering students to develop' (Wisker *et al.* 2008: 8). This chapter looks at three aspects of one-to-one teaching: the relationship between teacher and learner, the use of listening skills; and giving and receiving feedback.

Emotions and the teacher–learner relationship one-to-one

James Derounian and Wal Warmington investigated undergraduates' experience of dissertations and concluded that 'relationships do indeed lie at the heart of the dissertation process' (Derounian and Warmington 2007). Their findings suggest that 'the undergraduate dissertation is, for staff and students alike, a substantial and fraught undertaking', and is 'stressful and emotionally charged'. Comments from respondents in Tamsin Haggis's small-scale study of adult postgraduates included, 'the relationship with tutors has been the single most negative contribution to my learning experience here' (Haggis 2002: 214) and 'supervisors can be very undermining and damaging' (ibid.). Clearly the potential for the teacher's words and actions to influence the feelings of the learner is greater in one-to-one work than in a group, as the relationship between teacher and learner becomes more evident and therefore more significant.

Given the centrality of the teacher–learner relationship in working one-to-one, it is worth revisiting activity 2.1, which uses metaphors to enquire about the relationship of a teacher to a group. Here is a different set of metaphors for the one-to-one relationship. The task is the same.

1. Ask, which of the following metaphors best captures how you incline to relate to your learner?
    - Detective to suspect
    - Doctor to patient
    - Personal trainer to client
    - Radio interviewer to guest
    - Maestro to novice
    - Researcher to interviewee
    - Coach to athlete
    - Counsellor to client.

2. Now ask, how will that feel for the learner? In other words, how does it feel to be treated as a novice or as an interviewee or as an athlete and so on?

3. Finally, is this metaphor you have identified the best one for assisting the learner in their development?

If using emotional intelligence in your one-to-one teaching demands putting energy into developing a good relationship with your learner, adapting frameworks such as cooperative development and Nonviolent Communication (see Chapter 16) may be useful, because they both stress the importance of attending to the affective component of one-to-one exchanges by the careful, deliberate use of language.

Many of the activities in chapters 2 to 14 apply or can be adapted for working one-to-one, but the following are of particular relevance:

> Adapt activity 1.3 by considering how you would like your learner to feel at the end of the one-to-one exchange (the feelings listed in 1.3 are just examples). Once you have identified those feelings, ask, 'What do I currently do and say in order to encourage those feelings? Is there more that I could do or say?'

Activity 4.1 looks at the physical experience of the learner in group sessions, including the arrangement of furniture. Normally there will be an unavoidable power relationship between teacher and learner, especially where the teacher assesses the learner. Be wary of making this more evident in the one-to-one exchange by the arrangement of seating such as the teacher sitting behind a desk or sitting at a higher level than the learner.

Activity 8.5 is about the teacher attending not just to the factual content of a learner's email but also to the feelings conveyed, and preparing to respond accordingly. The same principles apply face-to-face. Be ready to listen, and to respond, to both facts and feelings.

Activity 9.3 looks at transactions between 'personal styles', which of course will be happening when you work one-to-one. The first step is to become conscious of such transactions and then to review the extent to which they are helpful to the relationship and to learning.

Activity 12.1 is about your non-verbal communication, which will be significant for your learner one-to-one, so monitor your tone of voice, facial expression, posture and so on.

Listening skills

Of course, the one preceding chapter which is wholly applicable in one-to-one exchanges, perhaps more so than in group teaching, is Chapter 7 with its focus on listening skills. If the goal of the teacher working one-to-one is, to use the verbs from the Wisker *et al.* quote above, to support, facilitate, enable and empower, the ability to genuinely listen to the learner becomes essential. Kristin Mason O'Connor and Lynn Oates, in their publication *Academic Tutoring* (Mason O'Connor and Oates 1999) present seven examples of responses by learners to the way tutorials are handled by the tutor. Here they are:

1. 'I know he really means to be helpful with his suggestions, but my tutor keeps telling me about how he would deal with things before I can even tell him properly what my problems are with the project.'
2. 'My tutor shares his office with two others. When they came into the room, he kept breaking into our tutorial to pass on messages to them. He also kept answering his phone.'
3. 'When I am having a tutorial with her, I feel as if I am being interrogated; it's quite frightening, really. You feel you have to try to work out what she wants to hear rather than what you think.'
4. 'I told my tutor that I had to select my modules to fit in with my job at Burgers-R-Us and she practically jumped down my throat telling me I was here to concentrate on getting my degree.'

5. 'I was up most of the night looking after my sick father but managed to get to my tutorial at just after 9.00 having just dropped off my son at the childminders. I was exhausted. I just clammed up when the tutor asked me to summarize the key points raised in the lecture. I felt terrible when she said crossly, "I don't know why I bother putting so much into preparing my lectures."'

6. 'I've more or less given up going to his tutorials as he seems to use it as an opportunity to finish off what he didn't get through in the lectures. As I get a bit lost in his lectures anyway, I don't want to spend more time getting more confused.'

7. 'I find her tutorials really stimulating: they certainly make you think. Time passes so quickly that it's always a surprise when she suddenly interrupts the discussion to tell me it's time to end.'

(adapted from Mason O'Connor and Oates 1999: 22-29)

I have used these examples with many groups of teachers and asked the question, 'In each case, what advice would you give to the academic tutor, given this learner's reaction?' Answers vary for each scenario, but most indicate that the teacher could listen more and listen better and in particular be more attentive and empathic. The results of not doing so in terms of the learners' feelings are evident and cannot be said to be conducive to learning.

Some active listening skills appropriate to work with groups of learners were presented in activity 7.1. Here is a fuller list, which can be used in the same way as in 7.1, but with a focus instead on your use of listening one-to-one.

non-verbal
communication other than through the words you use; including your posture, eye contact, tone of voice, facial expression
being attentive
listening attentively, and being aware of the effect of your own feelings and perceptions on what you hear
reflecting feelings
saying to the speaker what feelings they are communicating to you
paraphrasing
saying back to the speaker what they have just said; sometimes verbatim, sometimes using different words but retaining the meaning
use of questions
using questions, especially open questions, to help the speaker clarify their situation and explore their ideas more fully
summarizing
drawing together information, ideas and experience presented by the speaker
clarifying
checking your understanding of what the speaker is saying to you

challenging
helping the speaker to be more aware of what they are saying, by drawing their attention to inconsistencies and discrepancies in their statements and actions
managing silence
choosing, when the speaker stops speaking, not to take that as a cue for you to start speaking, but simply to remain fully attentive.

All of the above skills relate to observable behaviours except 'being attentive'. This is more about what is going on in your mind as you attempt to listen. If you have difficulty with this, here are some possible causes:

anxiety – It is difficult to give someone your complete attention if you are feeling tense and anxious. Anxiety might lead you to interrupt, jump in too quickly, offer advice, or withdraw and clam up. You will almost certainly be giving non-verbal signals that will make the learner tense and uncomfortable too. If this is you, pay attention to any clues as to what your anxiety is about.
lack of concentration – When you are very busy or have a lot on your mind, it is sometimes difficult to turn off your own preoccupations to give attention to someone else.
impatience – You may be the sort of person who likes to rush around getting things done. This, again, may lead you to jump in with practical suggestions and advice, or feel more comfortable talking yourself. Remember that what you are trying to do is to assist the learner to make their own decisions and find their own solutions. This may take a lot longer, but it is a very important part of the process.
desire to be in control – This is linked to anxiety and impatience and may be particularly relevant for teachers who are used to taking a lot of responsibility and decisions. Try to be aware of when, how and why you take control.
attitudes and prejudices – Revisit Chapter 12. We all have the potential to make assumptions about other people based on our own attitudes and prejudices. Check whether your ability to truly listen to your learner may be impeded by your response to their age, gender, accent, appearance and so on.

It's important too for you, in teaching one-to-one, to hit the right balance between facilitation and direction. Too much facilitation on your part could leave the learner feeling uncertain and adrift. Too much direction could encourage feelings of dependency and lack of confidence. Gerard Egan's three-stage model of helping (Egan 2010) can be a useful guide in achieving that balance, as it is initially person-centred but allows for advice and direction.

Feedback one-to-one

The remainder of this chapter focuses on feedback given by the teacher to the learner. Sara Varlander has written on the role of emotions for learners receiving feedback. Noting the effect that power and status dimensions have on emotions in social interactions, she suggests this is particularly important in teacher-to-learner feedback situations. 'In the tutor-student interaction, students often perceive a lack of power, and in feedback situations this power asymmetry may become especially pronounced' (Varlander 2008: 152). So teachers should 'strive to eliminate students' perceived power asymmetry, in order that students feel more confident in the interaction with the tutor' (ibid.) and should also attempt to develop empathy with learners in this situation, making the teacher more aware of 'students' anxieties relating to feedback situations' (ibid.). Strategies she suggests to achieve this include:

1. discussion with learners about feedback
2. making criteria explicit
3. providing guidance on how to give and receive feedback
4. seeking feedback on the feedback.

1. A discussion with learners about feedback before they receive any could affect their response to it. The discussion could touch on the role of feedback and its advantages and disadvantages and what it is intended to achieve.
2. Making criteria transparent could 'decrease insecurity and anxiety related to the feedback process' (ibid.: 153). If learners have a clear idea of what is expected of them, it does not remove their concerns about whether they can achieve that, but it should prevent anxieties that may arise from not knowing what is required.
3. Indicating how feedback should be given is essential if you are preparing learners for peer feedback. It can also help to discuss with learners good and bad experiences of feedback, to identify guidelines for improving the quality of the feedback and how it is given.
   To enhance the effectiveness of feedback, some preparation is needed on behalf of the recipient. Here are some guidelines that you can use or adapt for use with your learners on how to receive and make best use of verbal feedback:
   - Assume the feedback is going to be constructive and useful.
   - Put your energies into listening (rather than preparing a response).
   - Let the person giving the feedback finish.
   - Monitor your non-verbal and emotional responses.
   - If necessary, ask for clarification or for repetition.
   - Attempt to paraphrase what you have heard – say it back to the person.
   - Thank the person for the feedback.
   - Take time to evaluate the feedback.

- Take the time to think before making any response.
- Consider possible actions in light of the feedback.

4. Finally, Varlander suggests seeking feedback on the feedback in order to get learners' perspectives on how useful the feedback was and how they felt. Sarah Quinton and Teresa Smallbone (2010) asked learners to complete a 'Reflections on Feedback' form in order to assist them in reflecting on the feedback they received and to let the teachers know their response to it. The form has just three questions:

- What do I *feel* about this feedback?
- What do I *think* about this feedback?
- Based on this feedback what *actions* could I take to improve my work for another assignment?

(Ibid.: 129)

One copy of the completed sheet is retained by the learner, as a record of their action points. Learners have the option of leaving the other copy for the teachers.

Incidentally, the authors noted the most commonly recurring feelings recorded by learners about the feedback they received on coursework assignments. These included disappointed, irritated, gutted, upset, worried and saddened, alongside pleased, happy, relieved, motivated, satisfied and 'mixed emotions' (ibid.: 130).

When considering learners' responses to feedback, the work of Carole Dweck is useful. She has identified two different mindsets that people possess about themselves that affect their approach to learning and their response to success or failure. There is the 'fixed' mindset where you believe that your abilities are unchangeable and there is the 'growth' mindset, where you believe your abilities can be developed through effort (Dweck 2006: 6–7). If we attribute success or failure to factors beyond our control, as in the fixed mindset, we can become less motivated; if, as in the growth mindset, we attribute success or failure to factors in our control, we have the potential to become more motivated. Of course, this applies most when the learner is challenged or facing difficulty. Failure is interpreted differently, either as an identity (I am a failure) or as an action (I failed) (ibid.: 33).

Clearly a learner's emotional response to feedback may be influenced by their mindset, and Dweck indicates that mindsets can be changed. Geoff Petty suggests that feedback methods themselves can assist learners in changing from a fixed to a growth mindset. 'When students compare what they did with what they should have done they realise why marks were gained or lost, and that this is not to do with ability, but with doing it the right way' (Petty 2009: 46). In Mantz Yorke and Peter Knight's research, 25–30 per cent of samples of both students and staff in higher education tend towards a fixed mindset and 70–75 per cent towards a growth mindset (Yorke and Knight 2004: 29).

Chapter 16

Teaching with emotional intelligence with online learners

Most of this book is about face-to-face encounters between teachers and learners. The question is often asked, 'How far does the guidance on teaching with emotional intelligence apply with learning that is wholly online or with blended learning, which mixes online and face-to-face? Can the activities in the book be used or adapted or are different strategies needed?'

Emotions and online learning

Studies indicate that the emotional component of learning is present, sometimes very strongly, in learning online. Michalinos Zembylas, Mamas Theodorou and Andreas Pavlakis investigated the role of emotions for online learners. They gathered information from 92 adult learners on two Masters programmes over the academic year 2006–7 at the Open University of Cyprus. They reported that 'Positive and negative emotions related to online learning were the two broad themes that emerged from the data analysis' (Zembylas, Theodorou and Pavlakis 2008: 111). The three recurring positive emotions reported by learners were:

Excitement about the possibilities and flexibility of online learning, expressed as joy, enthusiasm and relief. (As the learners became better acquainted with the methodology of the course, their response became more ambivalent.)

Satisfaction in fulfilling course requirements. This stemmed from concerns by the learners, who were all in work, about meeting the demands of part-time study.

Excitement about online communication as they found, when they became engaged in it, that it increased optimism and reduced challenges. Some learners formed close relationships with others.

The negative emotions were:

Anxiety because of the unknown methodology of distance learning and the demands of the programme. They experienced distress and fear wondering if they would be able to cope.

Feelings of **loneliness and isolation** due to the absence of live chat, human communication and being aware of the burden on each of them to take responsibility for progressing with their studies.

Stress in case they were unable to fulfil other obligations – this was seen not as the result of the methodology of the programme but of the multiple roles the learners had to fulfil.

(Ibid.: 112–15)

Kerry O'Regan interviewed a smaller sample of learners studying online and identified the following as the most commonly occurring feelings:

Frustration
This was the most pervasive emotion. It was often about using the technology but was also in response to lack of clear instructions, the nature or structure of the online material, out of date materials and the unsatisfactory nature of unmoderated online discussion.

Fear, anxiety, apprehension
This resulted from delays in the system, exposure to an unknown audience, the public and permanent nature of online communication and confirmation of self-beliefs about difficulties with technology.

Shame/embarrassment
These feelings resulted from being exposed and feeling incompetent.

Enthusiasm/excitement
This stemmed from using new technology and connecting with people from around the country.

Pride
This positive feeling also resulted from the public nature and permanence of online communication.

(O'Regan 2003: 84–8)

Rosemary Lehman has written on the importance of 'presence' as critical to the success of teaching and learning at a distance using both synchronous and asynchronous technologies (Lehman 2006). Presence is a 'psychological state in which the technology becomes transparent to the user' (ibid.: 4) so that the user experiences an 'illusion of non-mediation' (ibid.: 3).

She suggests that emotions, as experienced by both learners and teachers, have a key role in shaping presence. She specifies 32 potential concerns in 'blended distance education' which could cause negative emotional responses such as confusion, frustration or fear, and she suggests how they could be addressed. The majority of these 32 items are clearly not exclusively about online learning. Examples include: learner expectations, trust, motivation, interest and attention. Equally, the factors that require attention by the teacher to prevent negative emotions are not distinctive to online learning. They include, for instance, ensuring robust course design, effective administration, opportunities for interaction, and clarity about aspects such as how the course operates and the respective roles of the teacher and learner. Many of the negative feelings experienced by learners appear to have the same source as in face-to-face encounters. The concerns that are clearly more significant in online learning relate to support and to the environment.

These three studies suggest that emotions are present for learners online and that they are significant, but that many of them stem from factors that are not unique to the online environment. It follows that some activities in the preceding chapters should be directly relevant to the experience of the online learner, with perhaps slight adaptation to the circumstances. This applies most obviously to activities in Chapter 5, 'Dealing with your learners' expectations'. Anticipating learners' fears (activity 5.1), ensuring an open exchange of information (activities 5.2 and 5.3) as well as airing expectations and/or negotiating rules about roles (activities 5.4, 5.5, 5.6) all have as much, if not more, significance for the online learner. These are particularly important for those learners unfamiliar with working online or who are anxious about the use of technology or the prospect of feeling isolated.

The facility to communicate online means that it is easier to deal with learners' expectations, exchange information, set the tone, allay fears and so on before the learning gets under way – you don't have to wait, as so often in face-to-face encounters, until the learners are assembling for a first meeting to attend to this. Strategies a teacher could use in advance of the course include:

- sending a welcoming email using the learner's name and encouraging contact from learners by email;
- arranging for a simple introductory forum which might be accompanied by a questionnaire where learners could discuss experiences, thoughts and feelings and share any concerns;
- recording a short audio or video welcome, which could include a mini guide to the course and a reminder of some of the key information. Even though this recording may simply repeat many of the written instructions that are also available, it does provide an alternative format and a more personal introduction to the course. This idea can be repeated on a regular basis and could be used to provide further explanations and support throughout the course.

Activities 3.2, 9.5 and 9.6 stress the care that is needed in the use of language, and this is particularly important online where, in the absence of non-verbal cues, words become more important. Gilly Salmon, in listing the qualities and competences required of e-moderators in computer-mediated conferencing, includes: 'able to write concise, energising, personable online messages' (Salmon 2000: 40). Finally, activity 8.5 is about reading and attributing importance to the feelings expressed in electronic communication, just as in face-to-face.

As so many of the strategies do translate, and when so many of the emotions triggered are the same, should online learning even be treated as a separate category in terms of teaching with emotional intelligence? I think the answer is yes, because there are components of the online learning experience which clearly differ from face-to-face teaching and that might affect the emotional responses of the learners. These components, which do overlap, are:

- the different environment;
- the necessity to engage with technology;
- differences in the nature of communication.

The online environment

Eva de Lera and colleagues at the Open University of Catalonia gathered data about the interaction between their learners and the online environment. Their conclusion was that more could be done to make the online learning environment engaging and motivating for their learners. They formulated 12 principles to guide initial design of the environment. They define this area as 'Affective Educational Technology', which:

> focuses on the design and assessment of affective educational technology in order to elicit favourable states for learning. Positioning our contribution within the affective loop, we especially focus on the first stage of design of environments that foster positive emotions in the learning experience. . . . The emotional dimension has to be visible in any of the spaces, tools or services that belong to the environment.
>
> (Fernandez and de Lera 2009: 3)

They stress that their focus is not on the design of engaging pedagogical methods, which are still important, but on 'the homepage, the community tools, the structure, design, functionalities and other elements of the virtual campus' (ibid.).

They offer these 'guidelines for designing engaging virtual learning environments':

1. **Personalization** – the environment must make the learner feel like a person and not like a user. Use communication strategies that are more personal, common language and options for this person to participate in this environment. The learner must have the possibility to design a personal learning environment.
2. **Identity** – utilizing real and consistent images to help the learner identify him/herself with the values and the community in a quicker and more efficient way, and so generating a sense of belonging.
3. **Brand** – ensuring that the brand and the brand values are reflected throughout the virtual environment to reinforce the relationship between the learner and the institution.

4. **Community** – offering options to communicate, relate and participate. Offering options to make friends, to gather in small groups and large groups and to promote associations. Making community options very visible and easily accessible.

5. **Surprise** – introducing positive surprise elements or special events in the initial entry pages or in strategic locations to make the learners feel that they are part of a creative and dynamic community, creating the idea that something is changing, something is moving, all of the time.

6. **Innovation** – integrating innovative elements in the virtual environment, those that they may begin hearing or reading about in the media.

7. **Zen** – ensuring that there is not an overload of text in the screen, that white spaces are used, as well as photographic or graphic elements.

8. **Search** – providing shortcuts to learners who have little time, ensuring that they can find the information they need by doing a simple search.

9. **Clarity** – utilizing lively and bright colours to facilitate interaction, reading and information visualization, providing guidance through the design.

10. **Situation** – ensuring that the learner quickly recognizes the structure or map of the environment in a glimpse, without needing to scroll or to read a lot.

11. **Aesthetics** – ensuring a consistent aesthetic throughout, to help guide the learner through his or her tasks and objectives.

12. **Recognition** – utilizing standard icons and symbols that can be easily and quickly understood without requiring the alternative text or an extra click to understand it.

(adapted from Fernandez and de Lera 2009: 4–5)

Using the technology

Kerry O'Regan indicates key areas relating to the technology that require attention. Discussing her findings she writes, 'In practical terms, implications can be based on the pragmatic assumption that learning will be enhanced when negative emotions are minimized and positive emotions maximized' (O'Regan 2003: 89). She suggests that, based on the experience of the students interviewed in her study, this is likely to occur when:

*   the technology is reliable, accessible and usable to the point of being invisible in its functioning. It should be acknowledged that this may still be an ideal, as the technology will for some time yet be prone to interruption, corruption or disruption;
*   instructions for accessing the required sites are clear, explicit, delivered up front, and make no unjustified assumptions as to students' knowledge and awareness of online processes;
*   sites are maintained and kept up to date;
*   content is designed to make explicit the structure of the material and to

facilitate the user's navigation through and awareness of location in that structure. Let learners know what to do on every screen;

- guidance is provided for appropriate, relevant and constructive participation in discussion groups; responsibility is taken for moderation and facilitation of discussion groups;
- posting and response processes are explicit, with students receiving prompt and automatic acknowledgment when postings are received;
- processes are put in place for students to have an indication of the actual make-up of the audience for any submissions they post online; provision is made for class members to become known to each other as real people with their own idiosyncratic interests and characteristics;
- where possible, online communication is augmented with face-to-face meetings if only for induction, to overcome much of the challenge of remote, distance learning.

(adapted from O'Regan 2003: 89)

Communication online

In the absence of body language or stress and tone of voice, online communication has the potential to be impoverished and to lead to more misunderstandings. This prospect may lead some learners to avoid communication, resulting in feeling more isolated, as the study of Zembylas *et al.* above showed. 'Cooperative development' and 'Nonviolent Communication' (NVC) are two frameworks that have been developed in separate contexts, but that are both designed to facilitate dialogue between two individuals that includes an affective component. Both have been experimented with in the online context to see whether they can still be effective.

Julian Edge has developed the framework of cooperative development for use in the professional development of teachers. It provides guidance for how one person (the Understander) can assist another (the Speaker) in reflective practice or action research. The Understander has five types of 'move' or response that they can make. These are:

> **Reflect** – check that they have heard and understood what the Speaker has said;
> **Relate** – bring to the attention of the Speaker two statements that the Speaker has made and see whether there is an interesting or useful relationship between them;
> **Focus** – help the Speaker move from the general to the specific in order to move towards action;
> **Set a goal** – help the Speaker articulate a goal for themselves;
> **Trial a procedure** – help the Speaker work out how they might work towards that goal.

(Edge 2006: 268–9)

The framework derives from Carl Rogers's work (see pages 66–7) and is also influenced by Gerard Egan's model of the 'Skilled Helper' (Egan 2010).

In 'Computer-mediated cooperative development: non-judgmental discourse in online environments' (2006), Edge investigates in detail the exchanges in two examples of using the framework in online communication. He does not identify 'any medium-specific effects on the Speaker/Understander dynamic, or on the development of the personal relationship involved' (ibid.: 224). Trust was developed and maintained between Speaker and Understander and, as in face-to-face exchanges, both reported benefit and satisfaction from their roles. Edge speculates that this might be the result of the 'professional purpose and formal clarity of these roles' (ibid.).

Elaine Cox and Patricia Dannahy looked at the use of Nonviolent Communication (NVC) in online coaching and mentoring (Cox and Dannahy 2005). NVC is especially relevant for use in situations where building relationships is key. It provides a framework for expressing and hearing affective information and can be used to create a suitable tone and to build rapport. It is based on the two people in an exchange using four steps. These are:

> **Observation** – what we are observing, expressed without evaluation or judgment;
> **Feelings** – what we are feeling in relation to what we are observing;
> **Needs** – what met or unmet needs lay behind those feelings;
> **Request**s – the request we would like to make in order either to stay connected with ourselves and others, or to meet our needs.
>
> (Cox and Dannahy 2005: 41)

In their research, Cox and Dannahy wanted to see whether NVC could be used in their online coaching and mentoring module, to 'provide some of the missing subtlety and sensory input lost over email' (ibid.). If communication comprises an information-giving component and an affective component, NVC should provide a means of accommodating both – information exchange through 'observations' and 'requests' and dialogue about feelings through 'feelings' and 'needs'. The authors found that the use of NVC in emails could speedily develop in-depth relationships between mentor and learners, paving the way for productive work on the learners' needs.

There are clear similarities between this account of the use of NVC and Julian Edge's work. Both use a structured framework to facilitate open communication between two people in which the affective dimension is explicit. The guidelines in both cases are about taking care with the exchanges you initiate, with the responses you make and particularly with your use of language, which is more important when the encounter is not face-to-face. Both report successful outcomes in electronic communication, albeit in small-scale studies.

This suggests that if the online teacher wants to make it more likely that learners have useful and supportive online exchanges with the teacher and between each other, it can help to offer explicit guidance on how to interact. The teacher can draw on frameworks such as the two above, which direct learners in how to communicate carefully with the intention of developing good, open online relationships. Such relationships can be a powerful tool in avoiding the feelings of isolation and anxiety which can affect the online learner.

Chapter 17

Teaching with emotional intelligence with international students

This chapter addresses the question which I am often asked: 'Do these ideas of teaching with emotional intelligence still apply and, if so, to what extent, when you are teaching international students?' I am taking the term 'international student' to refer to a student who has moved to another country to study full-time.

Emotions and international students

Of course, it is not correct to think of international students as a homogeneous group. In the words of Janette Ryan and Rosemary Viete, 'since international students (like domestic students) come from diverse cultural, economic, social, and linguistic backgrounds, they cannot unproblematically be characterized as having certain "qualities"' (Ryan and Viete 2009: 303–4). Even when students are all from the same country, individuals will have differing experiences of and perspectives on the culture and 'there can be as many differences within cultures as between them' (Trahar 2007: 15).

If a teacher recognized this and sought to understand better the culture of a student or a group of students by gathering information from them about their culture, that information might not be an accurate picture. It 'could reflect stereotypes that are blatantly untrue' argues Kam Louie (Louie 2005: 17). He goes on, 'Cultural knowledge is so fluid and constantly changing that it is impossible to "gather" it as if it were a pure and static thing' (ibid.: 23).

However, it is possible to talk about the feelings that international students are likely to have as a result of their experiences. These are in addition to feelings that may arise, such as anxiety or loneliness, from their situation of being away from home and because of what they have given up in order to study. Strong feelings can result from their experience of learning and teaching. Many such feelings reported by international students are documented by Janette Ryan and Rosemary Viete in their article, 'Respectful interactions: learning with international students in the English-speaking academy' (Ryan and Viete 2009).

International students report feeling powerless, excluded, ignored, isolated, marginalized, distanced, indignant and afraid. They may have feelings of disengagement, constraint and vulnerability. They can feel intense loss of self-esteem and loss of confidence. They report that 'I feel that they're ignoring me,' 'I'm not respected,' and they are described as suffering tribulations and frustrations (Ryan and Viete 2009).

It is important to stress that in all of the above examples, the feelings are a direct consequence of the students' experience of learning and teaching and often appear to stem from the perception, behaviour or words of the teacher.

Here are some of the common aspects of the international students' experience that prompt such feelings.

1. **Being seen as deficient, in varying ways**
   They may be seen as deficient in knowledge of the conventions and (often implicit) norms of higher education in their country of study. Sheila Trahar quotes Elizabeth Minnich, 'academics . . . can create particularly painful dilemmas for students from differing backgrounds, of differing turns of mind whose identities and loyalties are cast as liabilities from which they should liberate themselves' (Trahar 2007: 11).
   Also some teachers can see international students' language as deficient and then confuse the lack of proficiency in English with lack of ability.
2. A separate but linked occurrence is **not having their knowledge and experience valued**.
3. The international student can discover that **their fluency in everyday English does not necessarily equip them for understanding and using academic English**. 'Difficulties with language and unfamiliarity with concepts can present enormous obstacles for many students' (ibid.: 19).
4. Linked to this and also bound up with lack of knowledge of conventions for participation is the potential for experiencing **problems with participation in discussions and question-and-answer sessions**. Janette Ryan reports that many teachers saw international students as unwilling to participate in class discussion; and at the same time international students reported wanting to participate but needing help to do so (Ryan 2005: 93).
5. **They encounter new conventions for teacher–student relationships which can be confusing**.
6. They can experience **loss of self-esteem and identity**. Some descriptions from Christie *et al.*'s study (2008) of the experience of non-traditional students entering an elite UK university could equally apply to international students. They say that the transition 'involved the loss of a secure learning identity' (ibid.: 570); 'not knowing what standards were expected or how to undertake everyday learning activities, were bewildering experiences for many of the students' (ibid.: 572).

Teaching with emotional intelligence with international students

If teaching with emotional intelligence includes recognizing and responding to the feelings of your learners and encouraging an emotional state in the learners that is conducive to learning, in light of the above it is possible to suggest five strategies for teachers of international students. These are:

1. Develop self-awareness of your own culture, as well as of your own potential for stereotyping and seeing difference as less.
2. Plan for exchanges between you and your international students that include you explaining the conventions of your academic culture.
3. Develop and demonstrate empathy.
4. Be respectful and valuing of what your international students bring with them.
5. Reflect the possible needs of the international students in planning your learning and teaching strategies, especially with regard to language and participation.

1. Develop self-awareness

Glauco De Vita and Peter Case advise that in order to 'address issues of cross-cultural pedagogy' we should 'be more reflective about how we teach' (De Vita and Case 2003: 395). Teachers can often be unaware of the assumptions and conventions of their own academic culture; it is easy to take them for granted. There is the likelihood that our 'learning and teaching practices . . . are unexamined for cultural embeddedness' (Trahar 2007: 5). This includes aspects such as the role of the teacher, the role of the student, assessment grades, plagiarism, academic writing and so on. 'The more teachers are aware of their own culture, the more likely they are to be able to help international students adjust and thrive in the new academic culture they have (sometimes unwittingly) chosen to experience' (Carroll 2005: 34).

Jude Carroll provides a list of behaviours of international students, generated by teachers in British universities, in response to the question, 'What do international students do that you don't expect from home students? Are there any unexpected behaviours?' (ibid.: 29). The list is reproduced below. Take each item in turn, and ask yourself, 'What is the "invisible normal rule" (ibid.) that has been broken or ignored by these behaviours?' This activity should enable you to identify some of the conventions that may need to be made explicit to international students, if not to all of your students. Of course you may have your own examples of 'surprising' behaviour to add to the list.

- Giving presents
- Answering all my questions with 'yes'

- Calling me Dr X even when I have said 'call me John'
- Complaining about wasting time on seminars rather than me teaching
- Handing in 4000 words for an essay with a 2500 limit
- Writing very personal coursework with the main point on page 3 and lots of unnecessary background
- Repeating verbatim my lecture notes in the coursework
- Coming into my office after I have given the marks to argue loudly that I should give them higher marks – several times
- Remaining silent in seminars even when I ask a direct question
- Coming up after the lecture for a 1:1 discussion and seeming to expect me to stay for as long as it takes even though I said 'Any questions?' in the lecture
- Deferring to my opinion even when a preference would be appropriate (e.g. Me: 'Which essay will you do as coursework?' Student: 'Please, you say')
- Talking loudly in lectures.

(Carroll 2005: 29)

2. Plan for exchanges

Once you have been able to articulate for yourself the assumptions underpinning your academic culture, it may be easier to plan for how to facilitate 'exchange between students and tutors about the cultural values, assumptions, fears and hopes that are being brought to bear on the multicultural learning encounter' (De Vita and Case 2003: 391). It is important to explain to your students that you are aware that some of their expectations and assumptions may differ from yours and that the intention of any such exchange is to develop mutual understanding. Activity 5.6, 'Exchanging expectations' is well suited to this purpose, but of course can be adapted to whatever aspects of the students' experience of learning, teaching and assessment you think it is most useful to focus on.

3. Develop and demonstrate empathy

Kam Louie says that 'in the end, it is one's attitude and empathy towards the whole idea of cultural difference that matters' (Louie 2005: 17). Consider the situation of the international student. In particular, when you find their responses different, challenging or problematic, speculate on what lies behind this and what lies behind your reaction.

4. Be respectful and valuing

To be respectful and valuing of what international students bring with them can help to develop positive identities. It necessitates the use of listening skills (Chapter 7) and following the guidelines for responding to learners' comments and questions (Chapter 9).

5. Reflect the possible needs of the international students in planning your learning and teaching strategies

Take care in your use of language with international students without denying some of them the opportunity they are seeking to extend their knowledge of English and improve their proficiency. So:

- avoid or at least be cautious in your use of: slang, colloquialisms, acronyms, abbreviations, jargon, idioms, irony, and references that depend on cultural knowledge that students may not possess;
- take care not to speak too quickly;
- speak clearly;
- avoid the use of sentences which are unnecessarily long or complicated.

Some aspects of good practice when giving a lecture or talk become even more important, such as:

- providing a framework for each lecture, stating its main objectives, and how it links to previous and future topics;
- summarizing the main points of the lecture;
- 'flagging' important information through the use of phrases such as, 'this is a key point';
- pausing after key information or repeating or re-phrasing the information to allow more time for note-taking;
- providing lecture notes in advance or via the web.

(Ryan 2005: 97)

In giving reading, Sheila Trahar warns of overwhelming international students with a quantity of reading without direction, and so she advocates:

- highlighting highly recommended texts in a reading list;
- providing copies of essential reading;
- providing a list of questions to guide them through the reading of an article.

(Trahar 2007: 19, 21)

To encourage participation, assist international students in becoming 'able to communicate effectively, creatively and with confidence' (Ryan and Viete 2009: 309), by creating 'the contexts in which they feel safe and able to contribute' (ibid.). Take care in initiating and directing group work. Consider whether you want to direct the composition of groups in order to make it more likely that international students will contribute. Be explicit about the structure and process of any activity, in particular ensuring ground rules that will enable all students to have their turn to speak and to be heard and acknowledged.

Take particular care when handling questions or contributions from students whose first language is not English, because if these 'are difficult to understand or are unfamiliar, the tutor's body language or facial expression can sometimes betray a lack of understanding or acceptance' (Ryan 2005: 98).

Chapter 18

Continuing your development as an emotionally intelligent teacher

This chapter includes the following activities:

18.1 Self-assessment of your use of emotional intelligence in a session
18.2 Setting goals to develop your use of emotional intelligence in teaching
18.3 Storytelling
18.4 Reflecting on a session
18.5 Reflective diary
18.6 Pairing with a colleague
18.7 Learner feedback on your use of emotional intelligence

What does it mean and why does it matter?

This book, and in particular the activities in it, are intended to help you explore what using emotional intelligence can mean for you in your working context. Hopefully you have been assisted in starting to review and develop your practice in this area.

However, as stated earlier (chapters 1 and 10), the development of emotional intelligence and its use in teaching is by definition continuous. To be emotionally intelligent is to be constantly developing, to be forever enquiring about the feelings you observe in yourself and in others. Every encounter with learners has the potential for fresh experiences in handling the emotional dimension of learning. Remember too that this exploration cannot be confined to your role as a teacher; it is holistic and part of your continuing growth as a person. This final chapter suggests strategies to assist you in progressing your development as you continue to review and enhance your practice.

Formal opportunities to develop your use of emotional intelligence in teaching may present themselves. In addition to courses explicitly about the development of emotional intelligence, there are courses in, for instance, person-centred counselling or Transactional Analysis in education that touch on some of the areas covered in this book. In the absence of a formal course, the benefit of doing any activities such as those in this book will be enhanced if you are able to draw on another person, perhaps a colleague, to help you reflect and learn. Activities

18.3 and 18.5 below are examples of activities that depend on the help of others for their success.

The use of structured reflection as a tool for learning is common in professional development and is inseparable from the process of developing emotional intelligence. Just as emotional intelligence is essential for effective reflection, so the reflective process is essential in the development of emotional intelligence. Reflection is about learning from experience. In order to learn from experience it is invariably necessary to take account of the emotional component of the experience; Boud, Keogh and Walker (1985) see 'attending to feelings' as the second of the three stages of reflection. The starting point for the development of emotional intelligence is experience, and many of the activities in this book are designed to generate experiences for you to reflect on and learn from.

In the remainder of this chapter there are seven activities. Activity 18.1 provides a checklist of emotionally intelligent behaviours against which you can assess yourself, or be assessed by another, to review the extent to which you currently use emotional intelligence in your teaching, perhaps without giving it that name. Activity 18.2 suggests how to create action plans based on the findings of 18.1. Activities 18.3, 18.4 and 18.5 are three examples of how the reflective process may be used for your continuous development. Activity 18.6 outlines how to form an alliance with another colleague to aid your mutual development. Activity 18.7 suggests a means of obtaining feedback from your learners about your use of emotional intelligence.

Investigating your practice

Activity 18.1

Self-assessment of your use of emotional intelligence in a session

This activity provides a checklist of emotionally intelligent behaviours in the classroom, to use as a basis for identifying further development needs. Some of the 19 statements on the checklist can only be assessed by you, as they are 'internal' behaviours, e.g. 'monitor my prejudices towards any members of the group'. Others may be assessed by you and/or a colleague and/or your learners. Some of the items on the checklist lend themselves to being adapted for use in Activity 18.6. In 'Recognizing Emotional Intelligence in Professional Standards for Teaching: if emotionally intelligent teaching isn't on our standards agenda, is our ladder leaning against the wrong wall?' (2008), Eamonn Pugh includes an account of how he adapted this checklist for use with trainee teachers on teaching practice.

Complete the following checklist, which relates to your current classroom practice.

A = not at all   B = some of the time
C = all of the time   D = I'm not sure what this means

		A	B	C	D

To what extent do I

		A	B	C	D
1.	monitor my non-verbal communication and its effect?	☐	☐	☐	☐
2.	read learners' non-verbal communication?	☐	☐	☐	☐
3.	read the feelings of individuals?	☐	☐	☐	☐
4.	sense the mood of the group?	☐	☐	☐	☐
5.	respond to the mood of the group?	☐	☐	☐	☐
6.	convey empathy?	☐	☐	☐	☐
7.	give learners a chance to voice their feelings?	☐	☐	☐	☐
8.	**truly** hear what is being said by learners?	☐	☐	☐	☐
9.	acknowledge the presence of individual learners, verbally and/or by eye contact?	☐	☐	☐	☐
10.	acknowledge and value learners' responses?	☐	☐	☐	☐
11.	refer to individual contributions?	☐	☐	☐	☐
12.	ensure transparency about all the key information relating to the structure of the session, about what I expect and about what learners expect?	☐	☐	☐	☐
13.	acknowledge and manage my feelings during the session?	☐	☐	☐	☐
14.	convey my feelings to the learners, as appropriate?	☐	☐	☐	☐
15.	monitor my prejudices towards any members of the group?	☐	☐	☐	☐
16.	create a positive emotional environment?	☐	☐	☐	☐
17.	create the best physical environment in the circumstances?	☐	☐	☐	☐
18.	learn more about myself?	☐	☐	☐	☐
19.	learn more about the learners?	☐	☐	☐	☐

Developing your practice

Activity 18.2

Setting goals to develop your use of emotional intelligence in teaching

Use the checklist in Activity 18.1 as a starting point for setting goals. For example, select three 'A's or 'B's which you could do more often or at which you could be more accomplished. Turn them into goals, for example:

'I will make more statements to the group that convey empathy.'
'I will acknowledge the presence, by name, of each person in the room at least once in a session.'

For each goal you will need to decide:

- in which specific session you will start to make the changes
- what you would need to do and/or say additionally or differently, in detail, including the words you will use
- what preparation you will need for this
- what help, if any, you will need to prepare and go through with it
- what could go wrong
- what your contingency plan is.

Then you should write down the steps you need to take to carry out your plan, in sequence, with dates.

Activity 18.3

Storytelling

Turning your experiences into stories, which then form the vehicle for learning through reflection, can be a very powerful means of learning about the emotional dimension of your experience at work. As the activity indicates, you will need one person, or even better a small group of peers, to work with, and it is especially important that they are committed and able to fulfil their role in helping you make the most of the story.

Step 1

Choose an incident related to the emotional dimension of your work as a teacher that you want to explore further in order to learn from it. The incident may be one that you have not yet fully resolved, one that made you think about your practice, or simply one that you have never had the chance to talk about at length.

Step 2

Plan how you will tell your story, perhaps by writing it down.

Step 3

Brief your partner/group using the guidelines below on what you want them to do when you tell your story.

Step 4

Tell your story to your partner/group.

Step 5

Use your partner/group to help you explore your responses to what happened in the story.

Step 6

Attempt to draw conclusions from the story, both specific and general.

Step 7

Plan for how to deal better with, or to prevent, a similar incident.

Step 8

Imagine you had to write the story again, for a new audience. How might you find yourself telling it differently, following your storytelling experience?

For example, you might:

- include new details;
- emphasise different parts;
- include what you have learned;
- be clearer about the perspective of the others in the story;
- make it more of a comedy than a tragedy, or vice versa.

Guidelines for those listening to the story:

- Demonstrate that you are paying attention.
- Ask questions if you need clarification.
- Ask questions to prompt further reflection by the storyteller.

- Demonstrate to the storyteller that you have heard what is said and what is unsaid, both facts and feelings.
- Don't override the storyteller by relating your own experience or giving your own interpretation.
- Don't make judgements of, or offer opinions to, the storyteller.

For more extensive details on the use of storytelling in reflection, see *Learning through Storytelling in Higher Education* by Janice McDrury and Maxine Alterio (2003).

Activity 18.4

Reflecting on a session

To start your reflections on your teaching session, with an emphasis on teaching with emotional intelligence, complete the following unfinished sentences.

The feelings that I experienced during the session were

The feeling that I experienced most frequently or most intensely was

This was because

The most difficult/unwelcome feeling I encountered was

I felt best when

I would describe the mood of the group as

This could have been (even) better if

I was able to influence the emotional environment for the better by

One response/question from a learner that I could have handled better was

The area of teaching with emotional intelligence that I could develop next is

Activity 18.5

Reflective diary

Reflective diaries are a common vehicle for continuous professional development. This activity suggests three different focuses for diaries, each of which may be used to develop your use of emotional intelligence.

1. Incidents

Whenever you experience an incident that holds significance for you in the area of being a teacher or working with learners, use the following checklist to guide your reflective writing about it.

- What happened?
- What feelings were aroused in me?
- What did I have confirmed or find reassuring?
- What did I discover?
- What questions am I left with?
- What plans and resolutions will I make?

2. Relationships

Keep a regular diary, for example with weekly entries, which reviews how you relate to individual learners and groups of learners.

One way to get started on this is to revisit some of the material from Chapter 2. Alternatively, you could describe the strengths and weaknesses in your relationships with different groups or individuals. For example, what is it about some relationships that you find rewarding? What is it about other relationships that you find threatening?

3. Experiments

Whenever you try something new that is designed to incorporate emotional intelligence in your teaching, write about it. Use the same checklist as in 'Incidents' above.

Activity 18.6

Pairing with a colleague

This involves you and a colleague making an agreement about offering mutual support. The activity shows how a formal, structured approach can be adopted by two colleagues. Like storytelling, it provides a very potent means of exploring the strong emotions that may be bound up in work-related incidents. The agreement should sit alongside your relationship as colleagues and perhaps friends. It is an agreement to move to a more formal relationship when either of you requests it. However, it does not prevent the pair of you from having everyday discussions of problems in a less structured, more spontaneous way. As in Activity 18.3, the skills of the listener are vital in making it work.

1. Find a colleague whom you feel you can trust and with whom you can form a partnership to aid your mutual professional development.
2. You agree that at certain times either of you may draw on the other for help in solving a problem or exploring an issue.
3. If possible, arrange to meet on a regular basis and share the time available.

4. In any one session, decide who will be listener and who will be talker, or take, for example, half the session each, taking turns in each role. The roles work as follows:

Listener:

- pays attention;
- makes responses which:
    -   confirm they have heard fully what the talker has said;
    -   help the talker explore the issue thoroughly;
- allows the talker the time to explore the whole issue;
- tolerates very strong feelings expressed by the talker;
- seeks not to give guidance or advice (even when asked to) but rather assists the talker in finding their own solution;
- does not make judgements.

Talker:

- uses the attention of the listener to help them unravel the problem/issue;
- does not feel obliged to come up with a quick solution;
- is comfortable with revealing doubts or uncertainties.

Activity 18.7

Learner feedback on your use of emotional intelligence

Getting feedback from learners on your work as a teacher is good practice. Conventional feedback forms focus on important questions relating to materials, structure of the session, presentation and so on. This activity invites you to expand on the usual questions and find out a little more about your use of emotional intelligence.

Assume you are seeking feedback from learners at the end of your teaching session.

You have three standard open questions you use on the form:

1. How useful was the session?
2. What effect did it have on your work for this module?
3. Please comment on the quality of the materials and presentation.

You want to add three further questions to get some feedback on your use of emotional intelligence. Here are some of the things you might ask about:

- listening;
- empathizing;

- creating a climate;
- attending to feelings;
- being open about your feelings.

Many others are suggested by the titles of chapters in this book or by the checklist in Activity 18.1.

Here are examples of the kinds of question you might ask:

1. How fully did the teacher listen to comments and questions from the group?
2. How much did the teacher acknowledge individuals' presence and contributions?
3. Please use three words to describe the atmosphere in the room.

Think of three or more questions about your use of emotional intelligence that you would like answered.

1.

2.

3.

Conclusion and further reading

If you have found this book of use in your development as a teacher, I hope you will be able to continue exploring how the use of emotional intelligence can enhance your work. The book has been designed to aid your learning by practice and reflection, that is, by active learning. However, if you would like to explore further reading in this area, here are some suggestions, in the absence of other books specifically on emotional intelligence in teaching. (Full details of all titles are in the references that follow.)

Noam Austerlitz has edited *Unspoken Interactions: Exploring the unspoken dimension of learning and teaching in creative subjects*, which is an anthology of 12 papers by staff at the University of the Arts, London exploring emotions and social interactions within creative practice-based learning.

Attachment Theory and the Teacher–Student Relationship by Philip Riley uses adult attachment theory to examine teacher–student relationships, including how the attachment process influences teachers' and learners' emotional responses in the classroom. Although school teaching is its focus, there are implications for teaching in all sectors.

Empathic Intelligence: teaching, learning, relating by Roslyn Arnold explores how a readiness and ability to fuse the cognitive and affective is indispensable for exceptional teaching.

The Emotional Experience of Learning and Teaching by Isca Salzberger-Wittenberg, Gianna Henry and Elsie Osborne looks in detail at examples of how the hopes and fears of teachers and learners inform their interaction and relationships.

The Art of Changing the Brain by James E. Zull investigates, with many practical examples, how what is known about the workings of the brain can be used to make us better teachers; chapters 5 and 12 focus on the role of emotions.

Transactional Analysis for Trainers by Julie Hay goes into detail about how the theory of TA translates into practice for anyone responsible for groups of learners, whether you see yourself working in training or education. *TA Today* by Ian Stewart and Vann Joines is a thorough and accessible introduction to the many components of TA.

Parker J. Palmer's belief is that we must strive to be ourselves in our teaching. This authenticity is at the heart of what it means to be emotionally intelligent. He makes his case with compassion and elegance in *The Courage to Teach*; a 10th anniversary edition was published in 2007.

Freedom to Learn by Carl Rogers, originally published in 1967, captures his belief of the central importance of the relationship between teacher and learner.

For what emotional intelligence means in everyday life, Geetu Bharwaney's *Emotionally Intelligent Living* is a good introduction that includes an excellent short account of the history of the term.

I wrote in the conclusion to the first edition that we should replace René Descartes' words 'I think therefore I am' and begin to assert, 'I feel therefore I am.' In considering an alternative ending for this second edition, I wondered whether to use words attributed to the American author Maya Angelou: 'I've learned that people will forget what you said, people will forget what you did, but people will never forget how you made them feel.'

However, I do not want to cause distress to all of those teachers contemplating the prospect that no-one will remember anything they said or did, so instead I will end with the words that a participant wrote following a workshop I ran on teaching with emotional intelligence. The host institution's evaluation form ended with the question, 'What action will you take as a result of this workshop?' and one person wrote simply,

'Be more human'.

References

Arnold, R. (2005) *Empathic Intelligence: teaching, learning, relating*. Sydney: UNSW Press.

Aspy, D. and Roebuck, F. (1983) 'Researching person-centred issues in education: our research and our findings', in C. Rogers, *Freedom to Learn*, 199–217. Ohio: Merrill.

Austerlitz, N. (ed.) (2008) *Unspoken Interactions: Exploring the unspoken dimension of learning and teaching in creative subjects*. University of the Arts, London.

Beaty, L. and McGill, I. (2001) *Action Learning: A Practitioner's Guide*. London: Kogan Page.

Bharwaney, G. (2007) *Emotionally Intelligent Living*. Carmarthen: Crown House.

Boud, D., Keogh, R. and Walker, D. (1985) 'Promoting reflection in learning: a model', in D. Boud, R. Keogh and D. Walker (eds), *Reflection: Turning Experience into Learning*, 18–40. London: Kogan Page.

Brockbank, A. and McGill, I. (1998) *Facilitating Reflective Learning in Higher Education*. Buckingham: SRHE and OU Press.

Carroll, J. (2005) 'Strategies for becoming more explicit', in J. Carroll and J. Ryan (eds), *Teaching International Students*. Oxon: Routledge.

Carson, B. H. (1996) 'Thirty years of stories: the professor's place in student memories', *Change*, 28(6), 10–17.

Christie, H., Tett, L., Cree, V. E., Hounsell, J. and McCune, V. (2008) '"A real rollercoaster of emotions": learning to be a university student', *Studies in Higher Education*, 33(5), 567–81.

Claxton, G. (1999) *Wise Up: The Challenge of Lifelong Learning*. London: Bloomsbury.

Cox, E. and Dannahy, P. (2005) 'The value of openness in e-relationships: using Nonviolent Communication to guide online coaching and mentoring', *International Journal of Evidence Based Coaching and Mentoring*, 3(1), 39–51.

Cranton, P. and Carusetta, E. (2004) 'Developing authenticity as a transformative process', *Journal of Transformative Education*, 2(4), 276–93.

Crossman, J. (2007) 'The role of relationships and emotions in student perceptions of learning and assessment', *Higher Education Research & Development*, 26(3), 313–27.

Csikszentmihalyi, M. (1997) *Finding Flow, The Psychology of Engagement with Everyday Life*. New York: Basic Books.

Damasio, A. (1996) *Descartes' Error: Emotion, Reason and the Human Brain*. London: Papermac.

De Vita, G. and Case, P. (2003) 'Rethinking the internationalisation agenda in UK higher education', *Journal of Further and Higher Education*, 27(4), 383–98.

Derounian, J. and Warmington, W. 'Zen and the art of dissertation negotiation: How the student–staff relationship works', paper presented at the AISHE conference, Maynooth, Ireland, August 2007.

Dirkx, J. (2001) 'The power of feelings: Emotion, imagination, and the construction of meaning in adult education', *New Directions for Adult and Continuing Education*, 89: 63–72.

Dweck, C. (2006) *Mindset*. New York: Random House.

Ecclestone, K. and Hayes, D. (2009) *The Dangerous Rise of Therapeutic Education*. Oxon: Routledge.

Edge, J. (2006) 'Computer-mediated cooperative development: non-judgmental discourse in online environments', *Language Teaching Research*, 10(2), 205–27.

Egan, G. (2010) *The Skilled Helper: a problem-management and opportunity-development approach to helping*. Belmont, Ca: Thomson Brooks/Cole.

Elton, L. (1996) 'Strategies to enhance student motivation: a conceptual analysis', *Studies in Higher Education*, 21(1), 57–68.

Fernandez, C. and de Lera, E., 'Emotions, the forgotten key of success in Online Learning', paper presented at 13th UNESCO-APEID International Conference, Hangzhou, China, 2009.

Gardner, H. (1983) *Frames of Mind: The theory of multiple intelligences*. London: Heinemann.

Gardner, H. (1999) *Intelligence Reframed: Multiple Intelligences for the 21st Century*. New York: Basic Books.

Gardner, H. (2006) *Multiple Intelligences: new horizons*. New York: Basic Books.

Gilbert, F. (2004) *I'm a Teacher, Get Me out of Here!* London: Short Books.

Goleman, D. (1996) *Emotional Intelligence: Why it can matter more than IQ*. London: Bloomsbury.

Goleman, D. (1998) *Working with Emotional Intelligence*. London: Bloomsbury.

Haggis, T. (2002) 'Exploring the "black box" of process: a comparison of theoretical notions of the "adult learner" with accounts of postgraduate learning experience', *Studies in Higher Education*, 27(2), 207–20.

Harkin, J. (1998) 'Constructs used by vocational students in England to evaluate their teachers', *Journal of Vocational Education and Training*, 50(3), 339–53.

Hay, J. (2009) *Transactional Analysis for Trainers*. Watford: Sherwood Publishing.

Heron, J. (1982) *Education of the Affect*. British Postgraduate Medical Federation, University of London, with HPRP, University of Surrey.

Jensen, E. (1995) *The Learning Brain*. San Diego: The Brain Store.

Jensen, E. (1998) *Super Teaching*. San Diego: The Brain Store.

Lehman, R. (2006) 'The role of emotion in creating instructor and learner presence in the distance education experience', *Journal of Cognitive Affective Learning*, 2(2), 12–26.

Liston, D. (2003) 'The allure of beauty and the pain of injustice in learning and teaching'. in D. Liston and J. Garrison (eds), *Teaching, Caring, Loving and Learning*, 101–116. London: RoutledgeFalmer.

Louie, K. (2005) 'Gathering cultural knowledge: useful or use with care', in J. Carroll and J. Ryan (eds), *Teaching International Students*. Oxon: Routledge.

McDrury, J. and Alterio, M. (2003) *Learning through Storytelling in Higher Education*. London: Kogan Page.

Macfarlane, B. (2004) *Teaching with Integrity*. London: RoutledgeFalmer.

Mason O'Connor, K. and Oates, L. (1999) *Academic Tutoring*. Birmingham: SEDA.

Maynard, M. (2003) 'Coping with difficult participants', *Train the Trainer*, Issue 7.

Meyer, D. and Turner, J. (2002) 'Discovering emotion in classroom motivation research', *Educational Psychologist*, 37(2), 107–14.

Moore, S. and Kuol, N. (2007) 'Matters of the heart: exploring the emotional dimensions of educational experience in recollected accounts of excellent teaching', *International Journal for Academic Development*, 12(2), 87–98.

O'Brien, L. M. (2010) 'Caring in the ivory tower', *Teaching in Higher Education*, 15(1), 109–15.

O'Regan, K. (2003) 'Emotion and e-learning', *Journal of Asynchronous Learning Networks*, 7(3), 78–92.

Owen-Smith, P. (2008) 'Rescuing the affective: teaching the mind and the heart', *Journal of Cognitive Affective Learning*, 4(2), 31–3.

Palmer, P. J. (2007) *The Courage to Teach.* San Francisco: Jossey Bass.

Pert, C. (1999) *Molecules of Emotion.* New York: Touchstone.

Petty, G. (2009) *Evidence-based Teaching: A practical approach.* Cheltenham: Nelson Thornes.

Pugh, E. V. (2008) 'Recognising emotional intelligence in professional standards for teaching: if emotionally intelligent teaching isn't on our standards agenda, is our ladder leaning against the wrong wall?', *Practitioner Research in Higher Education*, 2(1), 3–12.

Quinton, S. and Smallbone, T. (2010) 'Feeding forward: using feedback to promote student reflection and learning – a teaching model', *Innovations in Education and Teaching International*, 47(1), 125–35.

Riley, P. (2011) *Attachment Theory and the Teacher–Student Relationship.* Oxon: Routledge.

Rogers, C. R. (1951) *Client-centred Therapy: Its Current Practice, Implications and Theory.* Boston: Houghton Mifflin.

Rogers, C. R. (1961) *On Becoming a Person.* London: Constable.

Rogers, C. R. (1983) *Freedom to Learn.* Ohio: Merrill.

Ryan, J. (2005) 'Improving teaching and learning practices for international students: implications for curriculum, pedagogy and assessment', in J. Carroll and J. Ryan (eds), *Teaching International Students.* Oxon: Routledge.

Ryan, J. and Viete, R. (2009) 'Respectful interactions: learning with international students in the English-speaking academy', *Teaching in Higher Education*, 14(3), 303–14.

Salmon, G. (2000) *E-moderating: the Key to Teaching and Learning Online.* London: Kogan Page.

Salovey, P. and Mayer, J. (1997) 'What is Emotional intelligence?' in P. Salovey and D. Sluyter (eds), *Emotional Development and Emotional Intelligence: Implications for Educators*, 3–31. New York: Basic Books.

Salzberger-Wittenberg, I., Henry, G. and Osborne, E. (1983) *The Emotional Experience of Learning and Teaching.* London: Routledge and Kegan Paul.

Sappington, T. E. (1984) 'Creating learning environments conducive to change: the role of fear/ safety in the adult learning process', *Innovative Higher Education*, 9(1), 19–29.

Seligman, M. (2006) *Learned Optimism.* USA: Vintage Books.

Stewart, I. and Joines, V. (1987) *TA Today: A New Introduction to Transactional Analysis.* Nottingham: Lifespace.

Thomas, L. (2002) 'Student retention in higher education: the role of institutional habitus', *Journal of Education Policy*, 17(4), 423–32.

Trahar, S. (2007) *Teaching and Learning: the International Higher Education Landscape.* Bristol: Escalate.

Varlander, S. (2008) 'The role of students' emotions in formal feedback situations', *Teaching in Higher Education*, 13(2), 145–56.

Weston, C. and McAlpine, L. (1998) 'How six outstanding math professors view teaching and learning: the importance of caring', *International Journal for Academic Development*, 33(2), 146–55.

White, J. (2004) *Howard Gardner: the Myth of Multiple Intelligences.* Institute of Education, University of London.

Wisker, G., Exley, K., Antoniou, M. and Ridley, P. (2008) *Working One-to-One with Students.* Oxon: Routledge.

Yorke, M. and Knight, P. (2004) 'Self-theories: some implications for teaching and learning in higher education', *Studies in Higher Education*, 29(1), 25–37.

Zembylas, M., Theodorou, M. and Pavlakis, A. (2008) 'The role of emotions in the experience of online learning: challenges and opportunities', *Educational Media International*, 45(2), 107–17.

Zull, James E. (2002) *The Art of Changing the Brain*. Virginia: Stylus.

Index